"I'm so grateful for Scott, his role in miss[...]ed-upside-down ways to follow Jesus. This book will provoke important, hope-filled conversations about how to keep finding our way to love and serve in Christ's name with our neighbors across the divides of money, power and culture."

Kent Annan, author of *Following Jesus Through the Eye of the Needle* and codirector of Haiti Partners

"As always Scott Bessenecker's writing is insightful, eclectic and generates new paradigms. A brilliant missions administrator with a track record of mobilizing thousands, he speaks with authority at that cataclysmic discontinuity between the power structures of older US missions built on capitalist business models, and the global explosion of indigenous and youth-driven missions. Always analyzing emergent structures, he aptly identifies numerous themes, trends, breakdowns and new directionalities that enter into the core of the massive shift in the style of missional community that has occurred this generation."

Viv Grigg, associate professor, Azusa Pacific University, and author of *Companion to the Poor*

"Once again Scott Bessenecker has pressed on one of Western evangelicalism's stress fractures. His precision with thought and word are unparalleled in both his diagnosis of the problem along with imaginative remedies for the solution. Truly a prophet of our times, Scott's vision and clarity come through page after page in *Overturning Tables.*"

Christopher L. Heuertz, founding partner of Gravity, a Center for Contemplative Activism, and author of *Unexpected Gifts: Discovering the Way of Community*

"These days everything must bear the weight of productivity, and as Scott Bessenecker points out, that creates a climate of narcissism, materialism and triviality. Overturning Tables does just what it says—it overturns the neatly set table of corporate, white individualism and challenges us to shed egos, acknowledge limitations, embrace cooperation and resolve together to look for authentic signs of the kind of human flourishing Christ came to offer us."

Michael Frost, author, *Incarnate*

"This author is one of the few in the world whose knowledge, actual experience and first-person passion merge in such a rare way that the result is an uncomfortable but strangely freeing glimpse of the path we have been on, the consequences of that path and a way ahead. Those who care about mission among the marginalized will appreciate the refreshing and disturbing blend of the historical, theological and pragmatic critique, and its Jesus-like perspective."

Randy White, executive director, FPU Center for Community Transformation, author *Encounter God in the City*

Overturning
TABLES

FREEING MISSIONS FROM THE
CHRISTIAN-INDUSTRIAL COMPLEX

Scott A. Bessenecker

IVP Books

An imprint of InterVarsity Press
Downers Grove, Illinois

InterVarsity Press
P.O. Box 1400, Downers Grove, IL 60515-1426
World Wide Web: www.ivpress.com
Email: email@ivpress.com

Cover design: Cindy Kiple
Interior design: Beth McGill

Images: Christ and the Temple Money Changers: Christ Driving the Money-Changers from the Temple by
    Benvenuto Tisi da Garofalo at the © Scottish National Gallery, Edinburgh. The Bridgeman Art Library
    Graph paper: © Krockodilius/iStockphoto
    Pencil drawings of George Leile and Betsey Stockton by Janine Bessenecker.
    Images of slave ship and doves by Gary Nauman.

ISBN 978-0-8308-3680-2 (print)
ISBN 978-0-8308-9676-9 (digital)

Printed in the United States of America ♾

Library of Congress Cataloging-in-Publication Data
A catalog record for this book is available from the Library of Congress.

P	21	20	19	18	17	16	15	14	13	12	11	10	9	8	7	6	5	4	3	2	1
Y	32	31	30	29	28	27	26	25	24	23	22	21	20	19	18	17	16	15	14		

To Philip

CONTENTS

PROLOGUE

Driving the Market Out of Christian Mission

At the end of 2013 Pope Francis released an exhortation he called *Evangelii Gaudium* (The Joy of the Gospel) decrying free market capitalism, which he described as an economy of exclusion and inequality. In doing so he stirred up a wasp's nest of criticism, with some pundits calling his capitalist critique "pure Marxism coming out of the mouth of the pope."[1] In the document Pope Francis states,

> some people continue to defend trickle-down theories which assume that economic growth, encouraged by a free market, will inevitably succeed in bringing about greater justice and inclusiveness in the world. This opinion, which has never been confirmed by the facts, expresses a crude and naïve trust in the goodness of those wielding economic power and in the sacralized workings of the prevailing economic system. Meanwhile, the excluded are still waiting.[2]

But such a critique is not surprising coming from this particular pope. As his predecessor, Pope Benedict XVI, pulled away from the Apostolic Palace in a Mercedes limousine, Francis pulled up in his 1984 Renault. In fact, Pope Francis chose not to live in the Apostolic Palace at all, but to reside in the far less ostentatious Casa Santa Marta, where visiting guests of the Vatican stay. Pope Francis has a longstanding relationship with the wastepickers of Buenos Aires, whom he fought alongside for better working conditions as archbishop. It is this view of life from the margins which motivates the pope to suspend bishops living in opulence and challenge the capitalist obsession with profit at the expense of his friends living on the economic fringe.

But is it really the place of a religious authority to address economic systems? Should popes simply keep to religious matters and leave economic theorizing to economists? Surely we would not take seriously economists who attempt to shape Christian theology. Why should theologians address economic theory?

But the practice of economics is profoundly theological. What is "thou shalt not steal" if not an implication of economic policy that embraces some form of private ownership? Therefore, the first economist was God. Large sections of the Hebrew Scriptures are devoted to addressing economic malpractice and serve to protect those at the bottom of the economic food chain.

> You shall not withhold the wages of poor and needy laborers, whether other Israelites or aliens who reside in your land in one of your towns. You shall pay them their wages daily before sunset, because they are poor and their livelihood depends on them; otherwise they might cry to the LORD against you, and you would incur guilt. (Deuteronomy 24:14-15)

The Hebrew Scriptures devote a good deal of attention to how economic transactions are to happen and what should be done if those transactions go awry. The means to acquire wealth (via land or labor) was strictly guarded in the law. Leviticus 25 outlines the process by which land and labor were to be released on a forty-nine-year cycle after having been acquired by others. Land acquisitions were to be returned to their original owners. Those who had been sold into bonded labor were to be set free. This policy—the Jubilee—acted as a hard reset in order to correct the ways that all economic systems produce wealth disparities over time if not regulated. The Jubilee, along with a loan forgiveness cycle that repeated every seven years (Deuteronomy 15), were among the many ways God displays concern for how we exchange our goods and services and safeguards against rampant wealth inequality.

Luke opens his Gospel with a political reference—a census conducted around the time of Jesus' birth. For the Gospel writers, the lines between economics, politics and spirituality did not exist. Or if they did exist, they were placed differently than they are for readers in the industrialized, democratic West. Jesus' political and economic activism is often lost upon those who live in societies where the private practice of faith and the public practice of citizenship are kept in strictly separate containers. We do not easily see how Christ's actions and teachings touch on larger economic or political structures. Because Jesus does not attack the Roman Emperor— on the contrary, he encourages giving to Caesar that which is Caesar's (Matthew 22:20-21; Mark 12:17; Luke 20:25)—and because Jesus appears to embrace the permanence of poverty ("the poor you will always have with you" [Matthew 26:11; Mark 14:7; John 12:8]), we assume that Jesus takes a passive approach to political and economic powers. "Leave them well enough alone," our Western ears seem to hear him telling us, "devote yourselves to private spiritual matters and those larger structural issues will work themselves out." Jesus appears to be more concerned with individual economic practice—almsgiving, for instance—than systemic economic concerns, like interest rates or minimum wage laws.

But the holistic Hebrew mindset and the radically different private-public or sacred-secular divides in the ancient Near East obscure our vision on this. Everyday existence in Palestine during Jesus' time would have been a sociopolitical, religio-economic experience, and teasing out what might be relegated to the individual and private, and what involves

The first economist was God.

the communal and public, would have been difficult. Those lines were either drawn in radically different places or did not exist as we think of them today. Religious structures, political structures and economic structures were hopelessly bound together, and Jesus engaged the whole power fabric made up of these forces on a regular basis.

Teachers of the law, Pharisees, Sadducees, scribes: these were not viewed in the sanctified and separate ways that we view spiritual vocations today—men and women with religious power but no widely recognized civil power. Religious leaders in Jesus' day were civic leaders and part of a religio-political ruling class. The Sanhedrin ruled with as much civil authority as they did religious authority. Roman civil authorities were often part of the religious elite. There was no separation of power between spiritual and civil in Jesus' day.

The Roman governor Pilate, King Herod and the Sanhedrin were all concerned about Jesus' claim on their all-encompassing power bases, and Jesus' trial involved each of these power bases. Luke tells us that John the Baptist was locked up by Herod, one of the many religio-political rulers of that time, as a result of John's public tirade against him. The Baptizer condemned Herod not only "because of Herodias, his brother's wife" but "because of all the evil things that Herod had done" (Luke 3:19). Doubtless John was condemning a wide variety of unjust and self-serving actions of Herod, who, after all, was a builder, like his father, and levied burdensome taxes on those under his realm. In Herod's territory there was only the very rich and the very poor.[3] Herod himself owned half of the land under his rule, and many were confined to poverty as a result of Herod's policies and the aristocratic families who possessed much of the property. So paranoid was Herod of John's public denunciations that Josephus claims he feared John might "raise a rebellion."[4] This fear of rebellion indicates that the condemnation of Herod was not limited to what we in the West might relegate to the sphere of personal holiness. Private and public, individual and social, political and religious, economic and spiritual were part of a unified whole.

If we want to separate the powers and structures in first-century Palestine and distinguish the political from the social or economic or religious, we would have a very difficult time. Were the teachers of the law religious teachers or civil lawyers? Yes. Was the Roman emperor viewed as a political leader or a religious deity? Yes. Was the high priesthood a political post or a sacerdotal post? Yes. Was commerce in Jerusalem controlled by the religious elite or by business leaders? Yes.[5] Were the elite families in Judea tied to political, economic or religious power? Yes.

The temple in Jerusalem represented an amalgam of religious, civic and economic powers. Festivals or high holy days might be similar to attending a citywide parade on a national holiday—an event orchestrated by leaders with responsibilities in civic and religious circles that brought together family, friends, fellow citizens and strangers to trade stories, enjoy fellowship, worship, and share meals. Few would have known how, had they cared, to differentiate between the parts of the festival that were religious and those we might be tempted to call secular. The word *secular* did not even appear until the 1300s. That's because before the late Middle Ages the *secular* did not exist. State power was religious as well as economic and social. Artificial walls had not yet been constructed, and so we cannot so easily discern with our Western spectacles where Jesus confronts political, social or economic powers.[6]

The fact that we separate faith from politics or economics is a new way to look at the world and is foreign to human history. Jesus never addressed religious power without also addressing the social, political and economic power bound together with it. If we are honest, even in our church-state separated world, political and economic power has spiritual significance, and spiritual power has political and economic significance. Try though we might, we cannot uncouple all the ways the powers are mingled.

> **Jesus never addressed religious power without also addressing the social, political and economic power bound together with it.**

JESUS VISITS WALL STREET

Only a handful of events are recorded by all four Gospel writers. The Synoptic writers, Matthew, Mark and Luke, appear to follow a common account. John, however, introduces a large body of unique stories. He told his readers, "there are also many other things that Jesus did; if every one of them were written down, I suppose that the world itself could not contain the books that would be written" (John 21:25). This may account for his departure from the material the other three writers used. Therefore, we must pay close attention to those places where all four Gospel writers record the same event. These incidents are central to all four writers' understanding of the nature and work of Christ.

Outside of the death and resurrection narrative, there are just five events the Gospel writers share in common. Four of these are (1) John's baptism, (2) the feeding of the five thousand, (3) Peter's profession of faith, and (4) Jesus' anointing by a sinful woman.[7] Each bears special significance to developing the biography of Christ in terms of his fulfillment of Jewish, messianic prophesies. The fifth event is the story of Jesus' entry into Jerusalem and his ejection of the marketplace that occupied the temple courts (Matthew 21:1-13; Mark 11:1-17; Luke 19:29-46; John 2:13-17; 12:12-19).[8] What is so central to our understanding of Jesus that this event is among the few stories shared by all four Gospels?

It would be difficult to understand Jesus' entry into Jerusalem and clearing of the temple without reference to the larger political, economic and religious structures surrounding this story. The prophecy of Zechariah is brought to mind for Matthew and John, the two writers who were present at the event:

> Rejoice greatly, O daughter Zion!
>   Shout aloud, O daughter Jerusalem!
> Lo, your king comes to you;
>   triumphant and victorious is he,
> humble and riding on a donkey,

on a colt, the foal of a donkey....

His dominion shall be from sea to sea,

and from the River to the ends of the earth. (Zechariah 9:9-10)

There is a political dimension to Jesus' entrance into the epicenter of Judean power. Jesus does not chastise the crowds who hail him as king because they are politicizing his ministry. In fact the ruling class is disturbed by these politically laced cries from the crowd, and they ask Jesus to defuse the situation by correcting them. Jesus refuses: "I tell you, if these were silent, the stones would shout out" (Luke 19:40).

No wonder the power holders were nervous. The crowds wielding palm branches were reenacting a scene from the Maccabean revolt about a century earlier when Simon marched into the citadel at Jerusalem and threw off the foreign oppressors, establishing a short-lived, free Jewish state and restoring worship at the temple, which had become paganized (1 Maccabees 13:49-51; 2 Maccabees 10:1-8). While it may be argued that the crowds had misconceptions about Jesus' kingdom, there is no mistaking the real threat that Jesus and his reign would mean for existing powers.

While Jesus' entrance into Jerusalem may have been laced with Maccabean political significance, Jesus had not come to reform and preserve temple worship. No, Jesus' first act after being hailed as heir to David's throne was to confront an economic stronghold.

Then Jesus entered the temple and drove out all who were selling and buying in the temple, and he overturned the tables of the money changers and the seats of those who sold doves. He said to them, "It is written,

'My house shall be called a house of prayer';

but you are making it a den of robbers."

The blind and the lame came to him in the temple, and he cured them. (Matthew 21:12-14)

Driving out those selling sacrificial animals and overturning the money changers' tables must not be seen as an attempt to restore the temple to its Solomonic glory. Jesus had prophesied to a Samaritan woman that worship would no longer be linked to the temple in Jerusalem: "The hour is coming when you will worship the Father neither on this mountain nor in Jerusalem" (John 4:21). Luke records that when Jesus entered Jerusalem, he wept over the city's coming destruction (Luke 19:41-44), which was accomplished in A.D. 70, and in which the temple was also completely destroyed (Matthew 24:1-2). Jesus knew that the temple was destined to be demolished; in fact, Jesus' statements about the temple's destruction were used to convict and crucify him (Matthew 26:61). No, Jesus was not concerned about the purification of worship at the temple. The kingdom he brings has no temple because "the Lord God the Almighty and the Lamb" are its temple (Revelation 21:22).

I don't want to underplay the exclusion Jesus addressed in clearing the temple courts. There is most certainly a worship element that Jesus is confronting in his challenge to the marketplace ruling the temple. The worship of all people was being displaced by greed. This is a serious affront to worship. The original blueprint for the temple did not include corralling women and Gentiles into separate courts, away from pious male Jews, but this segregation had emerged, and Jesus displays such zeal inside these courts of the excluded. The fracas created by driving out the businesses ultimately had the effect of opening up space for the "unclean" to enter. Directly after Jesus clears the marketplace "the blind and the lame came to him in the temple, and he cured them" (Matthew 21:14). But Jesus was not only concerned with restoring a space where "true worshipers will worship the Father in the Spirit and in truth, for they are the kind of worshipers the Father seeks" (John 4:23 NIV). He was also confronting another thread of power twisted together with the strands of authority ruling the region.

> **Jesus' first act after being hailed as heir to David's throne was to confront an economic stronghold.**

In essence, money changers served as banks, and anyone coming to Jerusalem from another part of the empire would need the services of these currency exchanges. These temple banks were the place to go regardless of your interest in worship. True, they traded money for the temple coinage, but their business would have provided opportunity for all kinds of money exchange. We know from Josephus and other historians that the high priestly families earned lucrative profits from the temple marketplace, which included these banks. Niell Hamilton, in his article "Temple Cleansing and Temple Bank," suggests that the temple bank housed the equivalent of more than three million dollars, much of it from the deposits of aristocratic families. By overturning the tables, Jesus had "suspended the whole economic function of the temple. . . . Such sovereign interference in the economic affairs of the temple must have been taken as a direct claim to be king."[9] The high priest Ananias was called "the great procurer of money," and historians claim that the temple was being "ruined by greed."[10] Matthew's and Mark's Gospels specifically recall Jesus overturning the "seats of those who sold doves." These vendors would have catered specifically to poor folk like Jesus' parents, who

Box seats to a house cleaning. Linocut by Gary Nauman.

purchased doves to consecrate their firstborn male child in that same spot some thirty years prior. One influential member of the Sanhedrin a few decades later addressed the price gouging of the poor occurring at the hands of those selling doves. He fixed a maximum price for doves at just 1 percent of their original purchase price, giving us some idea of the profiteering going on in the temple marketplace.[11]

German theologian and scholar Joachim Jeremias writes in his book *Jerusalem in the Time of Jesus* that one wife in the high priestly family of Boethus "was so pampered that she carpeted the whole distance from her house to the temple gate."[12] The temple treasurer post was often filled by members of the priestly aristocracy.[13] Like today, economic power had coalesced into the hands of a few elite families, making access to wealth quite difficult for anyone else. Ched Myers concludes that "it is the *ruling-class interests* in control of the commercial enterprises in the temple market that Jesus is attacking."[14]

The temple clearing was not only a worship corrective but an economic corrective that struck at the heart of a first-century Wall Street.

FOLLOWING JESUS IN THE MINISTRY OF OVERTURNING TABLES

Jesus said in John 14, "whoever believes in me will do the works I have been doing" (NIV). If we are to do the works Jesus did, then there is something very appropriate about a religious figure like Pope Francis confronting the economic powers that have become weighted toward the ruling classes. We are charged to imitate our Master, and while this book is not primarily about inserting the ethics of Christ into a capitalist mindset, it is about addressing the capitalist mindset that has inserted itself into Christ's church and its mission.

> The temple clearing was not only a worship corrective but an economic corrective that struck at the heart of a first-century Wall Street.

Five-star US Army general and outgoing president of the Unites States Dwight Eisenhower warned of an unholy alliance between military powers and the for-profit business forces when he popularized the term *military-industrial complex*.[15] The mutual benefit between war and profit would have "grave implications" if those bedfellows were allowed to dictate foreign policy. Today, I see similar grave implications regarding the ways that the church has uncritically adopted a corporate-style capitalist paradigm to inform and drive our mission. It is an invitation for principalities that bend toward exclusion to occupy the temple courts of the church—the creation of a Christian-Industrial Complex.

I sometimes feel like I have more questions than answers. But the disturbance Jesus created in the temple courts gives me some comfort on this account. I am unsure what Christ's actions accomplished in the way of introducing permanent change to the economic lordship of the ruling class families controlling first-century Palestine. But an unmistakable signal was sent to the economic and political power holders deeply invested in the temple marketplace. Jesus' actions may also have inspired believers regarding the very different kind of "bank" which they would create just a few years later. It was an economic cooperative in which there were no needy among them (Acts 2:44-45; 4:32-35). Overturning tables indicates what his kingdom is like, or more to the point, what his kingdom is not like. In Christ's kingdom the poor are not bilked for the rich to carpet their palaces. It is not a kingdom where eighty-five individuals possess more wealth than three billion people.[16] It is not a kingdom where devotion to God is leveraged for ruling-class profit or where commercial enterprise gets in the way of those seeking to draw near to God. And it is not a kingdom where the world of profit making overrules the world of prophet making.

So while I hope to draw from a few alternative pictures of a church and mission that have been freed from a corporate-styled capitalist mindset, I am primarily attempting to kick-start a discussion. Can we more clearly identify places in the church where the ethic of gaining the world has resulted in forfeiting our souls? Have we allowed ourselves and our structures to be overly influenced by the things that work well in the capitalist kingdom of this world but are toxic in the good-news-to-the-poor kingdom of God? Can our imaginations be released to create fresh struc-

tures and new ways of understanding money, people, church and the
kingdom mission?

THE END OF WORLD MISSIONS AS WE KNOW IT

When I travel, I usually stay with friends, so it is a rare occurrence to stay
in a hotel, especially a nice one. After more than twenty-five years of
walking alongside college students or friends who live in developing-world
slum communities, it is always a little bit of culture shock to enter a conference environment where most people are white (like me), male (like
me), middle-aged (like me) and wearing business attire (not like me). This
is sometimes the reality when I attend professional events with other
North American missionary leaders.

At one such gathering I was handed the typical conference handbag,
adorned with sponsoring company logos. This bag contained a couple of
magazines, a conference handbook, and twenty-five different brochures
and fliers that advertised goods and services for sale to those of us who lead
Christian missions. There were appeals in this bundle made by travel
agencies, insurance companies, publishers and translation services. But the
profession represented by more flyers and ads than any other single industry
in the bale of paper was the financial industry—financial planning companies offered their help, a couple of banks presented their appeal to handle
the cash flow of organizations at this conference, and a company or two
were selling their fundraising services. Any outsider who only saw the brochures in our conference handbag might conclude that this conference
must be designed for an industry in which money played a central role.

The demographic of most Protestant missionary conferences in the US
could be described as male, pale and frail. Conference agendas are peppered
with the stated value of making space for younger leaders as well as women
and minorities. But the demographic of the room, at least as I have observed
it over the last twenty-five years, has remained the same. The Southern Baptists, for instance, are among the most diverse Protestant denominations.
"Nearly 10,000 of the SBC's 46,000 churches are 'ethnic in some shape, form

or fashion,' making Southern Baptists by far the most ethnic convention in the nation."[17] Yet the number of black Southern Baptist missionaries from the US is only one-half of 1 percent, and of the 4,900 Southern Baptist missionaries only 423 (8.6%) are minorities.[18] This raises the question: is there something about how Protestant mission is shaped that makes it easier for white folk to enter and more difficult for others? Surely ethnic minorities are no less spiritually gifted or qualified for missionary service.

In February 2012, a historic celebration was held honoring the two hundredth anniversary of the sailing of the first American missionaries sent by a formalized, missionary-sending structure: the launch of the Protestant mission to Burma in 1812. The anniversary was commemorated with the forging of a new partnership between two major associations of Protestant mission agencies under a single, new conglomerate. In many respects, this was an appropriate date and venue to attempt to breathe new life into the North American Protestant missionary structure. Only I'm not convinced that the organizational foundation upon which Protestants have built our church and non-profit establishments is the right one.

There is something endemic within North American Protestant non-profit structures which, despite good faith efforts, have made it difficult for minorities to thrive. In 2012 the birthrate of minority Americans exceeded that of whites.[19] By 2043 American minorities will become a majority.[20] What will become of our predominantly white missionary organizations, which have not kept pace with the changing demographic? Furthermore, outside of a few organizational exceptions like Youth with a Mission, I have observed the greying of North American missionaries. I was speaking to a missionary recruiter from the Evangelical Free denomination who told me the average age of the freshly minted missionaries they send to the mission field is forty years old. Another mission agency executive confessed to me that the average age in his mission is fifty-three. Efforts to draw in younger leaders have, by and large, been ineffective. What began as a youth movement is now a middle-aged movement. Finally, fully half of the Christian population appears to lack the correct chromosome pairing for upper leadership in Protestant institutions. While making up half of the Christian population, females have encountered enormous boundaries in offering their leadership gifts to churches and mission organizations.[21]

Women, young people and ethnic minorities face momentous hurdles in achieving prominence in our current Protestant missionary structures. This is not because these populations are less qualified. There must be something in the design of our organizations. If it continues, I believe we will witness the end of world missions as we know it—at least the Western, corporate version of world missions that we have become accustomed to.

The Missionary Corporation

The commercial corporation, as a manifestation of capitalism, grew out of the trading companies of the 1600s. In these early commercial ventures, wealthy backers banded together in order to undertake costly overseas trading missions. This corporate structure to commercial trade proved extremely lucrative. Just eleven years after its birth, the British East India Company was earning a whopping 150 percent return for their investors.[22]

The advent of this limited liability corporation came into being with profit as the primary engine, driven by wealthy investors who funded the new entity. In England and in other Protestant countries of the seventeenth century, the investors were married to their government's desire for hegemony (economic and military). The resulting corporation was a new creature on the human landscape. No one person had to undertake the fabulous financial risk of overseas trade. It could be spread among many investors and supported by governments who loaned early corporations their military muscle.

Not only did the corporate form of capitalism limit the financial liability of investors, but it limited the investor's relational connection to employees, products, customers and business practices in ways that were not possible with a sole proprietorship. This relational dislocation is partly why the slave trade continued for so long. In corporate-styled capitalism it is the investors and their pursuit of profit that govern organizational decisions. Products and employees simply become means to an end. Boards of directors and executive officers are beholden to the investors' quest for profit, and employees are beholden to executives' need for productivity. It is this hierarchical system of investors, board members, executives and employees which has come to define the modern corporation.

In this organizational design, money is the central factor in decision making. Employees are valued mainly for their productivity. Demand can be manipulated by marketing, and consumers are seen exclusively through the lens of their ability to purchase the product. It is this corporate-styled approach to organization that has become the chief construct by which Protestants have come to execute their various missions, whether financial, religious or social (more on this in chapter 2).

Today, particularly in the West, one can barely distinguish a conference designed for Protestant pastors, church leaders or mission agency executives from a commercial convention for those dealing with data management, telecommunications or selling shower-curtain rings. Protestant church and mission have become corporate-shaped ventures. Our central offices, our reliance on money, our relationship with employees, the marketing of our mission and the ways we think about success are informed by corporate capitalism. It has become the commercially inspired foundation upon which we have built our structures.

This should hardly be surprising given that the corporate-shaped organizational structure has been the container into which we have pressed nearly all other social organizations, whether the Red Cross, Goodwill, Public Broadcasting, the United Way or the YMCA. Nearly all the places we work have assumed the outline of a commercial business enterprise. Even health care and public education, the last bastions of altruistic human service, are being conformed more and more by the for-profit, corporate paradigm. The global transformation of all means of organizing is nearly complete. The capitalist corporation has become the grand unifying theory for all human cooperation.

The corporate spell under which we have become entranced has serious downsides, especially for the ways we need to come together for purposes that may not be practical, profitable or popular. Not every good offered to society should be reduced to a consumable. Not every working relationship should be defined by an employer-employee contract, and not every connection with other entities should become a business partnership. Additionally, money should not be a key ingredient for getting all things done. We are more than the business we have become.

We are more than the business we have become.

This should be true especially among those who preach the coming of a kingdom that is good news to the poor—those without capital—a kingdom that only the childlike can enter, a kingdom in which the socially excluded, the morally polluted and the physically unsuited are welcomed and given seats of honor. The power holders in God's kingdom are those typically left out of systems that reward greed, exploitation, and the concentration of wealth, power and influence.

To be sure, there is something admirable about how capitalism encourages creativity and entrepreneurship. It is one of the things I love about the free market. We've also witnessed a growing trend of for-profit businesses that celebrate a "triple bottom line." This business approach concerns itself with more than simply maximizing profit. Triple bottom line organizations take into account social as well as environmental stakeholders in decision making.[23] In addition, social enterprise has become a commanding force in human flourishing. People are rediscovering ways to organize that are not primarily centered around generating profit or massive fundraising. These organizations may well be instructive to the church. Social entrepreneurs such as Muhammad Yunus, founder and manager of Grameen Bank, have much to contribute to those of us engaged in Christian ministry. But what I see in the Protestant world is not usually the innovative business practices of today's entrepreneurs but a carbon copy of the business world of twenty or more years ago.

To address the ways in which we have become slaves to a corporate worldview, I explore in this book various threads of the corporatization of the church and its mission. Chapter one will contrast the corporate structure of the first American mission agency with the American slaves who represent the earliest American missionaries. Chapter two deals with the roots of the marriage between Protestantism and a corporate-capitalist mindset. Chapter three grapples with the paralyzing centrality of funding in our models. Chapter four explores moving away from a product mentality to our mission and toward something more holistic. Chapter five will look at replacing the emphasis on privatization and individualism with a more communal approach. Chapter six will help us to bring those excluded by the corporate paradigm into the center of our life and mission. Chapter seven will highlight the critical need to move away from partnership as a carefully delineated business arrangement toward a more interdependent approach, and chapter eight will make a case for rejecting the metrics rooted in the corporate vision for numeric increase in exchange for signs of the arrival of the kingdom of God.

What I Am *Not* Saying

I presented at a missiological study center on the need to explore missionary-sending structures apart from the predominant corporate business model. It was a three-day event with a group of perhaps thirty mission and academic leaders. On the last day I finally had a chance to sit next to the dean of a prominent evangelical seminary. "I've not been able to speak to you this week because of how angry you have made me," she stated. Others at that event thought I had summarily dismissed an entire era of Protestant mission by challenging the prevailing paradigm. Responses to my blog posts or talks have been laced with anger, disappointment and a sense that I have attacked individuals or sacred and cherished concepts. I confess that I have been caught off-guard by such defensiveness and resentment among my Christian brothers and sisters. There is a sensitive nerve under the surface of this criticism which I do not fully understand. I am not sure why Christians, Protestant evangelicals in particular, feel so keenly the need to defend unregulated capitalism. Perhaps it is a belief that capitalism takes economic power out of the hands of the state and gives it to the people. Both capitalism and Protestantism were responses to elitism. But movements that set out to overthrow elitism only create new elite and new excluded. We must never tire of reform; it must remain the one constant in a world that beckons us toward calcification.

Capitalism and Protestantism were responses to elitism. But movements that set out to overthrow elitism only create new elite and new excluded.

The other landmine I sometimes encounter are those who think I'm critical of business as mission. Business as mission is an organizing theory in which the wealth-creating or visa-granting power of business is leveraged to get missionaries onto a mission field, and like any other method for engaging the kingdom of this world with the kingdom of God, it comes with its assets and liabilities. At its best, business as mission is a form of Christian social enterprise, which combines wealth-creating opportunities for communities trapped in poverty with news about Jesus and his power to rescue. At its worst it is merely a ruse to get into a country with no real intention for the business to become financially viable. But business as mission is not what I am addressing in this book; my concern is mission as business.

One reason that the corporate business model has become such a standard organizational model is that it mostly works. What's more, the economies on which the entire planet now operate are built on a vision for wealth creation and distribution based largely on a capitalist worldview. This is because most alternatives have

Business as mission is not what I am addressing in this book; my concern is mission as business.

failed so miserably. Like it or not, capitalism is the economic ideology by which the world produces and exchanges goods and services, and the corporation is not going away anytime soon. As much as capitalism may have created wealth disparity, feudalism was far worse, and the state-run communist experiments have failed. Managing resources carefully, economizing production costs, motivating workers, and growing the reach and impact of organizations has been aided by the capitalist paradigm. Not even the great communist bastions of China and the former USSR have been able to withstand the gravitational pull of the capitalist star, because it can be such a powerful generator to move things forward.

Since I am not primarily an economist but a mission practitioner, I cannot comment with any academic rigor about the suitability of capitalism as an economic engine. However, I hope my readers will afford me the privilege of examining the capitalist paradigm, particularly corporate-styled capitalism, as a religious engine.

In addition, I must give some up-front clarification regarding the costliness and sacrifice of the eighteenth- and nineteenth-century missionaries who laid down their lives and buried their spouses and children in foreign soil while organized around a corporate-styled mission structure. Throughout this book you will find a critique of the Western Protestant church and its mission. I shudder to think what one hundred years might bring in the way of criticism to the alternative forms of mission I promote in this book. We are all trapped in a mental and theological framework born out of a miniscule fragment of time and space. The eighteenth- and nineteenth-century clergy and missionaries, along with the structures that supported them, were just as much prisoners of their culture and era as I am of mine. But they were also people of faith and courage, progeny of the "hall of faith" recounted in Hebrews 11: "Others suffered mocking and flogging, and even chains and imprisonment. They were stoned to death, they were sawn in two, they were killed by the sword; they went about in skins of sheep and goats, destitute, persecuted, tormented—of whom the world was not worthy" (Hebrews 11:36-38). I honor the verve and sacrifice of missionaries long dead, most of whom have gotten a bum rap earned by a minority of their colleagues, and their positive impact has been obscured by the colonization, exploitation and ethnocentrism that had infected all powers in those days.

One sociologist, Robert Woodberry, embarked on a fourteen-year-long search for the connection between Protestant mission and the emergence of free, democratic states. His careful research was published in the *American Political Science Review* and won several distinguished awards.[24] The conclusion of his research, along with a dozen similar studies, corroborate some fascinating findings: where independent Protestant missionaries had a significant presence, free democratic states emerged. The research suggests that powerfully democratizing elements such as literacy, education for women, robust nongovernmental associations and economic development were key catalysts for democracy and were either wholly generated or strongly promoted by these missionaries.[25]

Still, prayerful and prophetic critique is a gift—a gift I reluctantly but painfully receive for myself and one that I issue to the church and its mission in this book. In one hundred years I suspect that the structural solutions I offer in this book will, by then, be as ill fitted as the corporate, for-profit business shape is to ministry today. I am not saying that no good has come of the predominant missionary structures of the past two hundred or more years. I am suggesting that the time has come to examine and adjust a historic Protestant church and mission paradigm, one that has been driven and executed by faithful but fallible people and which has run its course. We need a fresh vision for church and mission, driven and executed by today's faithful but fallible people, which come with new assets and new liabilities, and which will require its own examination and adjustment in time.

But let us first explore how the US Protestant missionary enterprise was conceived and incubated in the womb of an emerging capitalist world.

1

A TALE OF TWO MISSIONS

The Western Hemisphere in the late eighteenth century was convulsing. A slave revolt in Haiti plunged that French colony into civil war, the Austrian and Ottoman Empires were embroiled in war, France was in turmoil, and the colonies in America were asserting their independence. Revolutions reverberated around the Occident from Belgium on down through Latin America in the decades of the late eighteenth and early nineteenth centuries, radically changing the geopolitical landscape. The industrial revolution fed the rise of capitalism as a major world force, which shattered the boulders of wealth primarily held by families who governed the world, and sent pieces of mammon flying out into corporations—a relatively new entity on the landscape, different from individuals or from states. This new body comprised mostly men who knew how to take raw materials like cotton or iron, combine it with working class or slave labor, and turn a profit for themselves and their investors.

The birth of the modern American Protestant missionary society emerged out of the context of these convulsions and was indelibly marked by the political and economic landscape onto which it emerged.

Most early Protestant missionaries, both American and European, were immersed in the spirit of capitalism taking root in the West. The leaders that gave shape to American mission societies in the nineteenth century were business-minded men. Families like the Rockefellers, Carnegies, Vanderbilts and the Morgans invested heavily in their Protestant churches and in domestic and foreign missions. These wealthy philanthropists were builders of the great educational institutions out of which most Protestant missionaries came, and promoted a positive attitude toward the corporate worldview within American Protestantism.

Adoniram Judson attended what would become Brown University and graduated valedictorian in 1807. He joined a handful of other collegians at that time and forged a secret missionary society—the Society of the Brethren—with the intention of bringing the gospel to foreign lands. Judson was joined by Samuel Nott of Union College, Samuel Newell of Harvard, and Gordon Hall and Luther Rice of Williams College. A couple of key clergymen who supported the boys' desire to become missionaries determined that "if a foreign mission were to be anything but a pious hope, a foreign missionary organization had to be formed to popularize the idea, raise money, disburse it, select missionaries, assign them to stations, support them and supervise their activities."[1]

This was, after all, the way successful people got things done. At that time it was axiomatic that if someone had a passion to advance anything in foreign lands, even Christian mission, a corporation needed to be formed, complete with investors, boards of directors, executive officers, employees, recruiters and accountants. The result was a missionary corporation, a Christian version of the for-profit trading company. The eighteenth-century North American and European imagination had become enchanted by the lords of profit.

These well-educated young men seeking to be foreign missionaries presented themselves to the annual General Association of Congregational Churches on a New England afternoon full in bloom with foxgloves, geraniums and Canterbury bells in June 1810. Protestants had already been debating the rightness of sending foreign missionaries at all. "If God wants to save the heathen,"

> **The eighteenth-century North American and European imagination had become enchanted by the lords of profit.**

one Baptist pastor told the "father" of modern missions, William Carey, "he will do it without your help or mine!" That debate was beginning to be won by missionary advocates across Europe, and the Congregationalists in America were now coming on board with that conviction. But these young men could not simply be released and commissioned to pursue their passion without any structure. And the primary organizational construct these Congregational leaders were skilled at building was commercial businesses, so the sending structure was designed and referred to as a corporation.

Dr. Manasseh Cutler was the moderator of the assembly and an astute businessman. He and a dozen others "bought" the state of Ohio, displacing thousands of Native Americans. He knew how to build a corporation. This new Christian Missionary corporation would be called the American Board of Commissioners for Foreign Mission (ABCFM). The first two treasurers, Samuel Walley and Jeremiah Evarts, have been described as "shrewd Yankee Christian businessmen."[2] "If we are to be the instruments of doing anything worth mention for the church of God and the poor heathen," Evarts was heard to have said, "we must exhibit some of that enterprise which is observable in the conduct of worldly men."[3] The creation of the first formal American missions association was forged with all the business savvy that the "worldly men" of the early nineteenth century could muster.

To send these young men (most would procure wives, some just days before the journey) would require raising $6,000, or roughly $168,000 in today's dollars. The chief precedent for raising this kind of money was commercial investment for profit. Investors were slow to put their money behind this effort. Returns on their funds would be spiritual, not material, and a venture of this sort came with a good deal of risk. The society sent Judson to London to discover what he could from the London Missionary Society, which had already been in operation as a missionary corporation for fifteen years. Perhaps they would even be willing to fund the mission. The society in London, however, was already preparing to spend

£10,000 on their missionaries that year (£321,700 by today's reckoning, or nearly $500,000). They were not terribly interested in taking on the financial burden of a team of American missionaries, at least not without the English board of directors exercising governing control over the American mission. This was something the American board was loath to consider. After all, Americans had just freed themselves from the bondage of British control and were not about to put themselves under the yoke of a British missionary society. Still, the ABCFM wouldn't mind taking British funds for an American mission. You could say that the Americans wanted the "taxation" of the London Missionary Society without their representation.

The mission party finally shipped out to Asia in February 1812, just when United States declared war on Great Britain. As if war were not enough of a challenge, three employees of the American mission bailed out of the missionary corporation before even reaching Burma. Adoniram, his wife Ann, and Luther Rice had come under the conviction that the Congregationalists were wrong on the issue of baptism. So a new missionary corporation was erected to employ them, the General Missionary Convention of the Baptist Denomination.

Like the commercial pattern from which it was cut, the American missionary corporation was desperately dependent on the financial resources of external investors for success. A less corporatized alternative would have been to help the young missionaries obtain passage overseas via professional means or through immigration. Maybe, like the apostle Paul, a mixture of financial contributions and paid employment would have sufficed. Structurally, the investors wanted substantial control over the mission, refusing funds from the London Missionary Society for fear that this corporate entity would take over the American corporate mission. Finally, rather than allowing some freedom for the missionaries to determine policy, a denominational issue, much like a corporate policy, ended the employment contract. The Christian-Industrial Complex was under way.

THE LEILE MISSION

An African proverb says, "Until lions write their own history, tales of the hunt will always glorify the hunter." For centuries the story of the first American missionaries were written by and written about the white, Ivy League collegians in New England. Adoniram and Ann Judson have often been lauded as the first missionaries from the United States, and their place in history uncontested. Then in the 1960s Stetson University history professor E. A. Holmes wrote a shocking article for the *Baptist Quarterly* displacing that myth. It was the story of a freed black slave who went as a missionary to serve among slaves in Jamaica.

The thirty years between the end of the war for American independence and the start of the War of 1812 mark a grand exodus. British loyalists, black slaves and Native Americans hemorrhaged out of the country on retreating war ships.[4] Some fled to St. Augustine,

> "Until lions write their own history, tales of the hunt will always glorify the hunter."
> *African proverb*

Florida, others to Nova Scotia and some to London. Thousands immigrated to nearby Jamaica. These three decades also separate two radically different paradigms for American Protestant mission. In the efforts of these freed slaves an older and lighter missionary structure emerged. They were no less intentional or effective in establishing outposts of God's kingdom abroad than the collegians who departed thirty years later, but they were not the engine to which Protestants, by and large, chose to hitch their train.

One former slave swept up in the British exodus was a gifted preacher. George Leile's Loyalist master, Henry Sharp, had given him his freedom before the start of the Revolutionary War, and Leile was ordained to preach to slaves in South Carolina and Georgia. Leile won to faith the early patriarchs of black American Christianity. These were men who established some of the first black congregations in the United States, men like David George and Andrew Bryan. Bryan was one of only three black Baptist preachers to remain behind in Savannah, Georgia, as the

British retreated along with blacks who feared reenslavement. In staying, Bryan faced harassment, beatings and imprisonment at the hands of whites who detested him for having the sheer audacity of gathering blacks for worship.[5] Under the protection of the Union Jack, David George, along with nearly thirty-five hundred asylum-seeking slaves, fled the United States to Nova Scotia and later immigrated to Sierra Leone, where he led congregations of blacks fleeing the United States.

George Leile and his wife, Hannah, however, had their sights set on Ja-

George Leile, first American missionary. Pencil drawing by Janine Bessenecker.

maica. Events surrounding the Leiles could hardly be more different than the Judsons. In order to obtain passage to Jamaica for himself and his family, Leile indentured himself to a Colonel Moses Kirkland in the early 1780s. It was not just freedom from oppression that motivated men like Leile to indenture himself in order to immigrate, it was freedom *for* the oppressed—both spiritually and materially—which coursed through the souls of George and Hannah Leile. They had tasted both oppression and freedom, and they were eager to seek liberation for men and women in Jamaica who suffered under the fetters of spiritual and human bondage.

"Though supported by no church or denominational agency, he became the first Protestant missionary to go out from America to establish a foreign mission, ten years before William Carey set out from England."[6] E. A. Holmes rocked the Baptist world when he published "George Liele: Negro Slavery's Prophet of Deliverance." While a handful of college students in 1806 gathered under the shelter of a haystack during a thunderstorm to pray for the birth of a foreign missionary movement, George and Hannah Leile had already labored for more than two decades in Jamaica. Their burgeoning Christian community of Jamaican slaves was enduring a good deal of persecution at the hands of plantation owners. The lords of Jamaican commerce believed that the gospel was a subversive and dangerous notion if planted in the heads of their human chattel. Slaves might get the idea that they were created in the image of God and that they should be treated with dignity. They might even come under the perilous conviction that it was possible for black slaves to be equal members with whites in the body of Christ. The liberating message of the gospel might spawn the kind of revolution expressed by Haiti's slaves, who seized control of their island. E. A. Holmes notes that "the planters rightly felt that 'the message of freedom embodied in the Gospel of Salvation to all men endangered the social and economic foundations upon which depended the Institutions by which they maintained their livelihood.'"[7]

Self-educated and self-funded, the Leiles' experience forms another vision of how we might view and structure mission—a vision less like the impressive armor of King Saul and more like the five smooth stones and sling of the boy David. "Bi-vocational all his life, Liele would, without complaint, support himself, his wife and four children by whatever jobs he could find."[8] He and Hannah had a large vision of Christian mission. They would labor for the abolition of slavery while at the same time calling Jamaican slaves to the Christian faith. There was no governing board to direct their work, few outside investors to support it, and no denominational or corporate policies by which they could be measured. Nonetheless, Holmes writes:

> A man without formal education, he learned to read the Bible and became a preacher of such effectiveness that in seven years in Jamaica he had converted over 500 slaves to Christianity. Though born a Negro slave in Virginia about 1750, his illustrious service as a patriot and preacher served as a weighty influence in the abolition

of slavery in 1838 from his adopted land of Jamaica. When the first English Baptists missionary reached Jamaica in 1814 there were 8,000 Baptist converts. This number grew to 20,000 Baptists in 1832, much of which growth was accomplished despite persecution by English planters and the jailing of Liele and his followers by the government authorities.[9]

It may be fair to say that the Judsons and their missionary colleagues were the first college-educated Americans sent out by a formal missions society on an oceangoing vessel, organized with the help of businessmen and invested with funds from charitable contributions. But if the story of spreading the good news about Jesus Christ belongs only to the highly educated and the highly financed sent by the highly structured, then a good many missionaries would be blotted out of church history, including the "ordinary and unschooled" followers of Jesus in the book of Acts, who started the church's missionary enterprise two thousand years ago. The fact of the matter is that the mission of George and Hannah Leile had a lot more in common with the first disciples than did Adoniram and Ann Judson's mission. The first three hundred years of Christianity's spread across Europe, Asia and North Africa was accomplished via the efforts of slaves fleeing persecution by the empire and sent with very little in the way of money or structure.

MAJORITY WORLD RISING

The capitalist-industrial paradigm has stifled our imaginations for envisioning how church and mission might operate differently. It has obscured mission history, blinding us from appreciating models that have worked in the past, and that, incidentally, are working today in other parts of the world. With the rise of the Global South not only are we witnessing a massive shift in the cultural and national identities of the world's Christian population but we are seeing a remarkable upscaling of Christian missionary efforts rising from places like Nigeria, China and India to places in the West.

In the 1840s Welsh missionaries were sent to the state of Mizoram, India, to plant churches. Today, the descendants of those first converts are now being sent as missionaries to Wales, where the church is in steep decline. The Rev. Hmar Sangkhuma has stepped into the void of Presbyterian ministers in Wales and runs yoga classes for the elderly. Knowing something about living a life of simplicity in his homeland, Rev. Sangkhuma is attempting to breathe spiritual vitality into a materialistic and consumeristic society. "There is a perceived lack of relevance of Christianity to lives based on materialism," he says.[10] And so in the heart of a quickly secularizing Welsh society, which 150 years ago was robust enough to send missionaries to India, the great-great grandson of some early convert has returned to call the Welsh back to their first love. This is a parable of twenty-first-century mission—the missionaries and mission fields have begun to swap places, and some of the methods will need to shift as well. India, Nigeria and China will not be able to conduct mission as those of us in the West have done. They will need fresh sending structures that will allow their relatively poorer population to serve in mission.

This is not to say that the missionaries from Africa, Asia and Latin America are getting it right 100 percent of the time. In fact, those from culturally homogenous regions are as ethnocentric as Americans and Europeans, unable to disentangle what is a cultural accessory to the faith and what is core. As a matter of fact, after more than two hundred years of committing serious errors in mission, European and American mission organizations represent valuable assets to our brothers and sisters in the rest of the world. It is not so much the *content* of Western mission that I am challenging here; it is the *container* of Western mission I have a problem with (though some critique of the content will come in chapter 4). It is a container that works well in the world of sales and profits but not so well in the world of souls and prophets.

The conviction to spread the teachings of Jesus abroad is not exclusively owned by the rich and the middle class, or by those who thrive in highly structured organizations. There are also those who grew up in poverty and are most comfortable in freer, less-encumbered structures. People like Efren and Becky Roxas.

I first met Efren and Becky in 2006 when I was in Manila to train university students headed for the slums of Asia. The Roxases were incredibly

The conviction to spread the teachings of Jesus abroad is not exclusively owned by the rich and the middle class.

easy to like, and I was drawn to them as soon as we met. Becky, with her round face, infectious smile and laughing eyes, and Efren, with his mischievous humor and impish grin, were smart, spiritual and fun loving. On the eve of a great adventure of their own, they had come to talk to our students about life among those on the economic margins. The next day they left as missionaries being sent from the slums of Manila to the slums of Phnom Penh.

Both Becky and Efren grew up among the rural poor and, like so many, had come to the metropolis of Manila as young, single people to seek a better life for themselves. Efren was a gifted student and was accepted into a top college. He rose at 4 a.m. each morning in order to make his food for the day and slog through Manila traffic to make it to school by 7. After class Efren went directly to a job as a janitor in a hospital until his shift ended around 10 p.m. Life for so many of my intelligent and industrious friends living in poverty is filled with challenge. There is no financial safety net, no extra breathing room and no margin for error. Poverty has a grinding effect on one's soul. "The field of the poor may yield much food," the writer of Proverbs says, "but it is swept away through injustice" (Proverbs 13:23). Eventually Efren buckled under the pressure and began drinking and taking drugs to endure the challenges of a life on the margins. Efren does not count this as an acceptable excuse for drug abuse, but it is what it is—an easy and accessible form of escape that rich and poor alike indulge in order to cope.

As Efren's life was collapsing around him, he met Becky, who became a stabilizing force for him. Perhaps this was the rock which would help hold his life together, so the two of them married. Like so many of the poor families around them, Efren and Becky began having kids almost immediately after getting married, adding to life's complexities the challenges of child rearing. Efren was unable to shake his addictions. The crushing weight of poverty and raising a family continually beckoned him toward the familiar escape route he had become so accustomed to. At one point, finding her husband drunk once again after returning home from work, Becky stormed into their bedroom and emerged wielding a World War II vintage .30 caliber carbine. She pointed the weapon straight at Efren to show him she meant business. This had a remarkably sobering effect. Efren was shaken out of his stupor, leaped out a window and tore off down the alley. Becky, of course, is not a killer. She had unloaded the gun before turning it on her husband, but her message was unmistakable. Unfortunately the confrontation did little to produce a lasting effect. Efren was as trapped in his addictions as he was stuck in a cycle of poverty.

In a moment of despair Efren happened upon a TV preacher talking about the prodigal son, and he immediately recognized himself in the wayward young man. Efren encountered God that day, just as the prodigal encountered the patient and forgiving father. There in front of God and the TV, Efren experienced a true conversion—tears of sorrow and surrender, falling on his knees and raising his hand. It was the lowest and the most grounded moment of his life. When Becky saw the transformation he had undergone for a year, she too took the plunge into the Protestant faith.

The neighborhood church they attended was what some call a "health and wealth gospel" church. The pastor taught that if one had faith, pursued God and gave generously to the church, they would become financially self-sufficient and never be sick. This theology appears to be unique to Protestants. But the Roxases noticed that the pastor and the middle-class church members seemed to remain financially stable and healthy with no apparent relationship to their faith (or lack thereof) and behavior (whether just or unjust), while Efren, Becky and the poor believers around them never budged from their place of economic desperation—no matter how earnest their exercise of faith, sacrificial generosity and just living.

When a Christian from New Zealand moved into their slum community, the teaching Becky and Efren had received on the role of wealth in following Jesus was shaken. At first they were suspicious. Why would someone from a background of privilege and wealth choose to live among the poor in a developing world slum? But eventually they grew close to Hugh, this odd Protestant missionary from a radically different mission called Servants. Rather than seizing the wealth and health available to them in the West, Servants missionaries relocate to some of the poorest neighborhoods on earth, seeking to live much like their neighbors and often enduring the challenges and hardships their neighbors face. Christ came to us in our poverty without insulation or protection from our adversities, why should we not follow his example?

Eventually, Hugh asked Efren if he would lead one of the four church plants in the slums where he was working. Efren agreed, and for years now, the Roxases have been an integral part of remaining in the slums and spawning a variety of works dealing with the spiritual, emotional and economic demons that haunt urban poor communities. In 2006, supported by their friends in the slums, Efren and Becky relocated as missionaries with Servants to Phnom Penh, Cambodia, where they have lived and worked among urban poor Buddhists. The challenges of working in a foreign environment, learning a new language and being separated from family are as challenging for Becky and Efren as they are for any Western missionary. A little support from the West and help from their friends in the slums have allowed them to serve for twenty-one years as Christian workers in a slum in Manila and for seven years in a Cambodian slum, largely without the elaborate machinery that many Western Protestant missionaries operate. The apostolic, missional life overseas is possible for the poor as well.

WE NEED A NEW MODEL

As we take another step forward in twenty-first-century mission, the weight of the church is shifting from one foot to another. The foot on which Christian mission has stood for the past few centuries is stretched behind us, and the foot on which we will soon be standing is out in front. It is no longer the wealthy, educated people of European descent who will be leading the missionary effort. The US missionary community continues to grow, but that growth is slowing. The European missionary effort is in decline while the missionary movements in Asia, Africa and Latin America are picking up. The Brazilians, for instance, now have more crosscultural missionaries than the Brits.[11]

In table 1 we observe the shift in the top twenty missionary-sending nations as a percentage of the Christian population over the period 1970 to 2010.[12] Five of the top twenty sending nations in 1970 dropped off the chart because they no longer send enough missionaries as a percentage of their Christian population: Portugal, Switzerland, Austria, Sweden and Bolivia. They were replaced by five countries that have moved up the list because of the dramatic increase in the number missionaries they now send: South Korea, South Africa, Philippines, China and Nigeria. The table can be slightly misleading due to a rapidly declining Christian population, giving some a positive change in the ratio of missionaries to Christians. Likewise, a country like India has more than doubled the missionaries sent in 2010 over 1970. However, India reflects a negative percentage change because the Christian population increased so much more dramatically. Nonetheless we witness in these numbers one window on the changing state of mission.

Majority-world missionaries are rediscovering what George Leile and the Christians in the first few centuries of the church knew instinctively— advancing the kingdom of God is not reserved for wealthy, well-connected or formally educated people; nor does it need to be propped up by a large and highly structured Christian-Industrial Complex. Some of these new missionary-sending nations are overturning the tables of our corporate-shaped ventures, though it is important to note that many are simply copying the business approach to mission of the Western missionaries who planted the church in these countries. This makes it all the more imperative that we begin to inspire newly shaped and newly resourced structures that can be more easily adopted by these emerging Christian communities.

Table 1. Top Twenty Mission-Sending Countries, 1970–2010, by Percentage Increase

Country	Missionaries sent per million Christians		% change
	1970	2010	1970 to 2010
China	0	47	
South Korea	13	410	3,015%
Brazil	27	191	613%
South Africa	394	1,904	384%
Nigeria	16	50	214%
Philippines	34	71	105%
United States	299	509	70%
United Kingdom	209	334	60%
Colombia	72	88	22%
Mexico	40	49	20%
Sweden	306	336	10%
Germany	237	241	2%
France	539	504	-6%
India	191	177	-7%
Austria	256	230	-10%
Belgium	1,048	913	-13%
Bolivia	403	341	-16%
Australia	331	257	-22%
Portugal	505	363	-28%
Canada	502	359	-29%
Switzerland	464	318	-31%
Spain	845	515	-39%
Netherlands	897	475	-47%
Ireland	555	190	-66%
Italy	4,406	1,253	-72%

Source: Todd M. Johnson, ed., World Christian Database (Boston: Brill, 2013).

Note: Missionaries are foreign missionaries who go to other countries. All Christian traditions are included (Catholic, Protestant, etc.).

(Bold font highlights the 5 countries that were not in the top 20 in 1970, but are in the top 20 in 2010.)

Protestantism is in decline in the so-called developed countries of the West. The percentage of Protestants in the United States has dipped below 50 percent for the first time since religious affiliation data has been collected in America.[13] It appears to be following closely the trajectory of other traditionally Protestant, Western nations like Great Britain, Australia and New Zealand. Most Western Protestant mission agencies employ highly educated, middle-class white people with access to capital. But even those of us embedded in middle-class American culture are finding it increasingly difficult to raise the large sums required to get onto the mission field. The era of the missionary corporation is drawing to a close.

What we need now are refreshed forms of mission. One history lover said the farther back you look the farther ahead you can see. Therefore, in the coming pages I will draw from older models whose picture and

The era of the missionary corporation is drawing to a close.

memory have been obscured by the prevailing corporate missionary-sending lens we have been seeing mission through for at least two hundred years. I will also explore more recent models of mission from communities like the ones sending Efren and Becky Roxas. These are Christian fellowships who use different mission methodologies than those of us in the Protestant West. These new missionaries are re-sourcing their mission in ways that do not lean on the copious amounts of money required by the existing corporate worldview. They are re-defining mission with a perspective that moves us away from a product orientation toward one that is more holistic. They are repopulating mission out of their naturally communal understanding of the faith rather than an overly individualistic interpretation of Christianity. They are reorienting mission toward a biblical view that leans away from the patron-client model and toward a posture of interdependence. And they are recalibrating mission through practices that defy the simplistic capitalist growth metrics that depend so heavily on dubious quantitative measurements.

But to drive the marketplace out of Protestant church and mission, we must trace the source back even further than the Judson mission of 1812. In the early days of the British East India Company we get a glimpse of the marriage between commerce and mission.

2

FROM CORPORATION TO
LOCALLY OWNED

While still in her mid-twenties, Queen Elizabeth had inherited a nearly bankrupt country and a seriously inferior military. She turned to a group of swashbuckling men of valor for help—men referred to as Elizabeth's Merchant Adventurers. They undertook incredible risks to lead commercial ventures abroad. Men like Sir Walter Raleigh and Sir Frances Drake helped to gain England's global supremacy at sea while building the national treasury through a kind of royally sanctioned piracy. Here we find some of the earliest touch points between the capitalist corporation and the Protestant faith, for it was through Protestant believers like Queen Elizabeth and her merchant captains that the trading company came into being.

Some may question whether the Queen and her adventurers were truly followers of Jesus. But reading some of the Queen's prayers we find a genuine sincerity of conversion.

> In the depth of my misery I know no help, O Lord, but the height of Thy mercy, who hast sent Thine only Son into the world to save sinners. This God of my life and life of my soul, the King of all comfort, is my only refuge. For His sake therefore, to whom Thou hast given all power, and wilt deny no petition, hear my prayers. Turn Thy face from my sins, O Lord, and Thine eyes to Thy handi-

work. Create a clean heart, and renew a right spirit within me. Order my steps in Thy word, that no wickedness have dominion over me; make me obedient to Thy will, and delight in Thy law. Grant me grace to live godly and to govern justly, that so living to please Thee, and reigning to serve Thee I may ever glorify Thee, the Father of all goodness and mercy, to whom with Thy dear Son, my only Saviour, and the Holy Ghost my Sanctifier, three Persons and one God: be all praise, dominion and power, world without end, amen.[1]

Some of the Queen's merchant adventurers were also zealous for their Protestant faith. Sir Francis Drake, for instance, is said to have won to the faith shipmate Michael Morgan while on a Caribbean voyage. Drake's father was a vicar in Upchurch, passing on to him a passion for the faith. And so it was through a Protestant queen, Protestant captains and Protestant investors that international commercial trade took flight.

Merchant ships invested with the Queen's own wealth and given sole rights to operate as a monopoly were sent to conduct trade at sea. They not only carried merchandise like the textiles of southern England, but they were equipped with heavy artillery and were more often than not staffed by a crew of ruffians who had been lured onboard with the promise of plunder. And plunder they received, forcing trade through the barrel of a canon with poorly defended ports in Africa, Asia and the Americas, and raiding Portuguese, French and Spanish traders of their cargo whenever the opportunity availed itself.

One such merchant adventurer was Sir John Hawkins. Like Elizabeth, Hawkins was a devout Protestant and liked to use a pious benediction with his men: "Serve God daily, love one another, preserve your victuals, beware of fire, and keep good company." Commissioned by the Queen and financed by a sterling list of what was London's rich and famous, Hawkins and his small fleet of ships arrived off the coast of West Africa on November 29, 1564, to gather their merchandise.

Hawkins had arrived at Cape Verde and had sent his men into the dense jungle in small raiding parties to hunt for slaves. The richest pickings were at the island of Sambula, where the slaves who were captured had been enslaved by another African tribe, the Sambolses, nearly three years earlier. Hawkins congratulated himself on a good beginning. So far, the "harvesting" operation had gone well.[2]

Weeks later, on December 25, Hawkins purchased two small shiploads of slaves from Portuguese traders, a Christmas present to himself and his investors. In the quest for profit on this early international, commercial voyage, four hundred slaves were packed aboard the 700-ton flagship, ironically named *Jesus of Lubeck*. Hawkins, though a professed believer, did not associate slave trading with immorality. In fact, in addition to the *Jesus*, his other two slave ships were christened the *Angel* and the *Grace of God*. The *Jesus* carried this human cargo in its belly across the ocean until, for three sultry weeks, the ship stalled in becalmed mid-Atlantic waters. Slaves began to die in the stinking, sweltering hold. One of Hawkins's officers described the conditions on a similar slaving mission:

> Not even a waist cloth can be permitted among slaves aboard ship, since clothing even so light would breed disease. To ward off death I ordered that at daylight the Negroes should be taken in squads of twenty and given a salt-bath by the hose pipe. . . . And when they were carried below, trained slaves received them one by one, and laying each creature on his side, packed the next against him, and so on, till, like so many spoons packed away, they fitted onto one another, a living mass.[3]

It is either a strange paradox or an act of profound redemption that the descendants of some of those slaves who were carried aboard a commercial vessel sanctioned by a Protestant queen and captained by a Protestant sailor should become some of the first Protestant missionaries. But the Protestant Reformation had coincided with the birth of the great oceangoing vessels like *Jesus of Lubeck*, which could carry hundreds of tons of goods. They were galleons, carracks and caravels, massive sailing ships that greatly accelerated intercontinental exchange—whether the exchange of cannon fire, merchandise or religious ideas. In comparison with overland travel, these ships exponentially increased both the risk and the profit of international trade. In cargo holds of these ships, international capitalism took flight in the form of joint stock trading companies. Whether dealing in spices, textiles, opium or slaves, the notion that people other than monarchs could take part in the profits of intercontinental trade was largely due to Protestant traders and a Protestant vision of creating personal wealth by leveraging private capital.[4]

Catholic nations also engaged in international colonization and trade, but these were either state-run or papal-sponsored ventures, not private ones. The idea of gathering investors and forming a corporation to make a profit from overseas trade appears to have been a concept that took root much more vigorously on Protestant rather than on Catholic soil, so it is not surprising to discover that from very early on Protestant missions were fused with corporate ventures like the slaving missions of Sir John Hawkins.

Luther on the Capitalist Ethic

German sociologist, philosopher and political economist Max Weber was among the first to point out the capitalist-Protestant fusion in his monumental book of 1904–1905, *The Protestant Ethic and the Spirit of Capitalism*. There was a variety of conditions in Protestantism that seemed to allow capitalism to flourish. For Weber, the spirit of capitalism was not so much the pursuit of greed as it was the pursuit of profit.

> Unlimited greed for gain is not the least identical with capitalism, and is still less its spirit. Capitalism may even be identical with the restraint, or at least a rational tempering of this irrational impulse. But capitalism is identical with the pursuit of profit, and forever renewed profit, by means of continuous, rational, capitalistic enterprise.[5]

Weber's understanding of Protestantism, or more accurately, Calvinism, is that making a profit because of thrift and industry reflects your goodness or even your godliness. Therefore the accumulation of money is a sign of "the elect," evidenced by working hard, spending little, accumulating much and not allowing money to sit idle. Predestination was one motivator, according to Weber, for the Calvinist to work hard. Since one's eternal election was unknown, godly virtues such as hard work were confidence builders that one was chosen for salvation and actively engaged in the process of sanctification.

Capitalism has too little traction in societies where people are satisfied with daily bread and choose to enjoy time with family and friends over working longer to earn a larger profit. Capitalist societies require the desire for profit at the expense of other things in order to thrive. Working hard and investing idle wealth were moralized in Protestantism, and this Protestant work ethic provided the engine for capitalism to spread. It is not so much capitalism which I find fault with in its marriage to Protestantism. But the limited liability corporation has serious drawbacks when used as an organizational container for churches and ministries. One key problem with this style of organization is how it fosters a hierarchical power structure between investors, board, executives, employees and customers.

Jesus was and will always be a people's Savior, and if his kingdom introduces any form of elevating one kind of person over another it is the kind of person excluded from the elitism the world creates based on power and wealth. The first missionaries were, for the most part, "unschooled, ordinary men" (Acts 4:13 NIV); they were relatively poor, and what wealth they may have held was sometimes held in common. There was little in the way of power dynamics between the individuals and churches that financed early mission, the apostles who traveled and the people who received them. If I could put a twist on Weber's essay I would not write about the Protestant ethic and the spirit of capitalism but about the capitalist ethic and the spirit of Protestantism. The spirit of Protestantism, as I see it, is access to God for everyone, the elimination of spiritual hierarchy. And the capitalist ethic is imbedded in the pursuit of profit at all costs, particularly in the form of the corporation. The corporate model tends most often to benefit those with enough excess wealth to be an investor. The elitism imbedded in the capitalist ethic, or at least the corporate vision of capitalism, is at odds with the spirit of Protestantism. Protestant churches and mission ought to animate structures that are economically lean and easily allow the poor to serve as missionaries, resisting the creation of a professional missionary class occupied almost exclusively by middle class, formally educated individuals. The spirit of Protestantism ought to find the ethic of corporate capitalism incongruous with the Christian worldview, with the corporations' tendency to concentrate power into the hands of those who already possess capital, its tendency to exploit cheap labor and its invigoration of consumerism.

Jesus was and will always be a people's Savior.

In the early days of the Reformation, Luther witnessed the dangerous undercurrents of commercially driven capitalism and cautioned Christians against allowing this worldview to run amuck in society. Trafficking in money, particularly expressed in the charging of interest or profiteering, was considered by Luther spiritually and societally hazardous.

In his 1524 treatise on trade and usury, Luther begins by confessing his doubt that his words and warnings will do any good in stemming the tide of greed fueled by the lust for profit. Even by the sixteenth century the profit quest had begun wreaking havoc on the Christian ethic of simplicity and contentment with daily bread.

> I think, to be sure, that this book of mine will be quite in vain, because the mischief has gone so far and has completely got the upper hand in all lands; and because those who understand the Gospel ought to be able in such easy, external things to let their own conscience be judge of what is proper and what is not. Nevertheless I

have been urged and begged to touch upon these financial misdoings and to expose some of them, so that even though the majority may not want to do right, some, if only a few, may yet be delivered from the gaping jaws of avarice. For it must be that among the merchants, as among other people, there are some who belong to Christ and would rather be poor with God than rich with the devil, as says Psalm 37:16, "Better is the little that the righteous hath than the great possessions of the godless." For their sake, then, we must speak out.[6]

And touch upon financial misdoings Luther does, though his suspicion that this would do no good was quite accurate. The Reformer went on to denounce how one person's desperate need will inspire a merchant to raise prices far beyond what it cost to produce the item. Where is the motivation to serve the need of the buyer out of a spirit of love or concern or Christian charity? "Charge what the market will bear" may seem like a harmless description of amoral market forces, but it is a damning adage according to Luther.

First—The merchants have among themselves one common rule, which is their chief maxim and the basis of all their sharp practices. They say: I may sell my goods as dear as I can. This they think their right. Lo, that is giving place to avarice and opening every door and window to hell. What does it mean? Only this: "I care nothing about my neighbor; so long as I have my profit and satisfy my greed, what affair is it of mine if it does my neighbor ten injuries at once?" There you see how shamelessly this maxim flies squarely in the face not only of Christian love, but of natural law. Now what good is there in trade? How can it be without sin when such injustice is the chief maxim and the rule of the whole business?[7]

If Luther could have foreseen the ways in which honest and compassionate Christian business practice might serve to employ so many, he may have been less bombastic. It wasn't that he was averse to profit. Luther reckons that using the price of a day-laborer's wage to determine how much a person should charge for his time is a good rule of thumb in determining profit margin. A modest amount might also be assumed for risk or for the possibility of an off year. But that a day would come when Christian ministry executives would make ten times more than the laborers who work for them,[8] or that companies run by devout followers of Christ would so depress wages or inflate prices as to make massive profits,[9] could not have been imagined by Luther. Nor could he imagine the engine of the capitalist corporation becoming the predominating structural paradigm by which his spiritual progeny would engage mission.

Steeping himself in the works of Max Weber and others, the socially minded Anglican Christian R. H. Tawney began to wrestle with the implications of capitalism. He did so from the perspective of his religious convictions as a Protestant. Tawney believed that in the two-hundred-year span between 1500 and 1700, the business world had become divorced from any kind of ethical accountability and had morphed into a morally bankrupt game of pure mathematical increase. Speaking about the removal of the church from participation in economic governance after the Reformation, Tawney says that "the ground which is vacated by the Christian moralist is quickly occupied by theorists of another order," and that Christians who previously felt there were moral rules governing their economic transactions have been swept into "the new science of Political Arithmetic, which asserts, at first with hesitation and then with confidence, that no moral rule beyond the letter of the law exists."[10]

THE COLONIZATION OF THE CHURCH

It was not just that early Protestant missionaries began catching a ride with commercial shipping operations like the British East India Company. Transportation options were limited at the time, and international travel was owned by commercial and political interests. It was that the very structure of the trading company became the pattern out of which the Western missionary cloth was cut. Missiologist Timothy Tennent says of

William Carey, cited by some to be the father of modern missions,[11] "Carey, as a Protestant rejecting the Catholic, monastic forms of mission, had no ecclesiastical structures to look to for guidance. So, he proposed a mission society based largely upon the model of secular trading societies, which were being organized for commercial purposes."[12]

And so it was that Protestants were not only the architects and financiers of modern, corporate-styled capitalism, they also adopted the corporate mold of the trading company as the template for mission's organizational shape. Missiologist Orlando Costas states, "Both Melanchthon and Zwingli, Calvin and Bucer held that mission work was the responsibility of the civil authorities. Therefore it does not surprise us that Protestant mission work began with the political and economic expansion of such Protestant countries as Holland, England, and Denmark."[13]

Catholic mission, by contrast, was far more political than it was commercial. David Bosch notes that Catholic mission was "based on the medieval assumption that the pope held supreme authority over the entire globe, including the pagan world. . . . Colonialism and [Christian] mission, as a matter of course, were interdependent; the right to have colonies carried with it the duty to Christianize the colonized."[14] In fact our word *mission* does not originate from Scriptures. While the term *sent one* (Greek, *apostellō*) was used to describe those disciples who intentionally traveled announcing good news, their work was not referred to as a mission. It is a word which comes from a sordid past and is about as helpful to the church today as the word *crusade* is for Christians working among Muslims. So mission was born out of the exploitative, sixteenth-century economic and political quest to acquire land, labor and raw materials, and to leverage them either for Catholic kings or Protestant investors.

> The new word, "mission," is historically linked indissolubly with the colonial era and with the idea of a magisterial commissioning. . . . The church was understood as a legal institution which had the right to entrust its "mission" to secular powers and to a corps of

"specialists"—priests or religious. "Mission" meant the activities by which the Western ecclesiastical system was extended into the rest of the world.[15]

The concept of Protestant mission, rooted as it is in the colonization of non-European lands, carries on its shoulders a hint of conquest, exploitation and imperialism. So as Catholic mission became inexorably bound to political colonization, Protestant mission found itself entangled with economic colonization. God's desire for his people to spread abroad his invitation to a new and glorious kingdom, where sinners receive forgiveness, the blind receive sight, the oppressed receive freedom and the poor receive good news of a better life, was tainted by the vision of economic gain through exploitation as well and the state vision for political hegemony.

British and Dutch Protestants each developed their own East India Companies as investment opportunities, vehicles for the rich to take advantage of the winds of trade that commercial shipping afforded. The Dutch East India Company was explicitly engaged in Christian mission, founding its own missionary training school and contracting missionaries to join their commercial ventures. Dutch missionaries were compensated by the East India Company for each baptism that they performed.[16]

The English investors, by contrast, were at first opposed to combining mission with commerce, not because they had theological problems with the notion but because their efforts to control or exploit the populations where they had planted their flags might begin to appreciate the liberty afforded all those made in God's image and then exercise that liberty. Eventually the British East India Company succumbed to Parliamentary pressures and accepted missionaries as part of their colonization vision. The commercial enterprises were to work hand-in-glove with the missionaries who had been sanctioned by the government to conduct mission in the colonies. Religious mission and economic mission were to run on parallel tracks. "When, in 1648, Parliament decided to take care of mission work separately, it created a mission corporation, a company with limited liability, the Society for the Propagation of the Gospel in New England. This was the model that would characterize most modern mission work."[17]

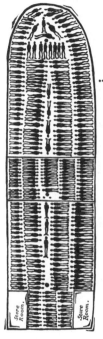

THE ENGLISH INVESTORS...
...WERE AT FIRST OPPOSED TO
COMBINING MISSION WITH
COMMERCE, NOT BECAUSE
THEY HAD THEOLOGICAL
PROBLEMS WITH THE
NOTION, BUT BECAUSE
THEIR EFFORTS TO CONTROL
OR EXPLOIT *the* POPULATIONS
IN WHICH THEY HAD PLANTED THEIR
FLAGS MIGHT BEGIN TO
APPRECIATE THE LIBERTY
AFFORDED ALL THOSE
MADE IN GOD'S IMAGE
& THEN EXERCISE
THAT LIBERTY.

To set the captives free. Linocut by Gary Nauman.

The colonial enterprise worked best if the European people at the helm could operate in a European culture housed within a European edifice. This required an unshakable conviction that European culture was superior to anything offered by the "natives" among whom they had come to do business. So to colonize meant necessarily having to reproduce miniature European outposts inside the borders of Africa, Asia and the Americas. The resources required to construct European cities within civilizations that had developed differently, with different sets of values, along different lines of thinking and with different kinds of materials, was fabulous. To do so was an organizational feat of monumental proportions, far greater a challenge than adopting or modifying the indigenous operating systems and buildings. But re-creating a European environment run on European values was how it must be if one believed European culture to be superior. Thus the commercial vision of establishing a beachhead on foreign soil included embedding a colony, complete with a critical mass of European people who could live European lives with all the conveniences (material and cultural) of Europe. This structure required colonists willing to transplant themselves in a foreign country. To do this meant re-creating their European lives with as little disturbance as possible. So when European and American missionaries translated this organizational paradigm into their vision for expanding God's kingdom, it took the shape of a mission society run by a board of mostly wealthy philanthropists and businessmen sending Western clergy and missionaries to live within a missionary compound patterned after their homelands.

THE COMMERCIAL MISSION TO KOREA

American missionaries to Korea in the late 1800s, taking their cues from the political and economic colonies of the British and American empires, created compounds that mirrored life in their home country. Since housing was most often supplied by the mission, this left them with disposable income relatively higher than other expatriates, and far above the Koreans they lived among. One missionary reflects that "compared with the Vanderbilts we live in a humble, not to say mean, way. Compared with the bulk of our constituents at home we live in, to say the least, the greatest ease and comfort. Compared with the people who, we have come to serve, we live like princes and millionaires."[18]

This was a far cry from the Christian wayfarers of the early church, and it was significantly different from the French Catholic missionaries who preceded the Protestants and were living in the harsh conditions of the local Koreans. Since missionaries were the only foreigners allowed to live permanently in the interior of Korea, relatively wealthy Protestant

American missionaries are attributed with generating demand for Western appliances and convenience items that otherwise would have been unknown to Koreans living outside of port cities. Interest in the goods that adorned Protestant American missionary homes began to surge. At times missionaries even became direct suppliers of this merchandise, angering company salesmen whose living depended on making such sales.[19] In 1897 the US Consular General to Korea charged in his trade report,

> The missionaries are very successful in their work and are held in high esteem by the people. They also do a great deal of good in the matter of the introduction of foreign goods and creating a demand for them. Of late, however, a very reprehensible custom had grown up among them of taking agencies for certain lines of goods, to the detriment of our merchants. Having their living assured and having no expenses, they can, of course, undersell the regular merchants. This causes much friction and brings the missionaries under the suspicion of too great interest in acquiring a money profit. I am sure the practice works to the injury of the mission cause.[20]

An entry in the Annual Report of the American Board of Commissioners for Foreign Mission suggests that mission boards were called on to act as advisers for commercial interests.

> We are asked to advise men as to commercial prospects in heathen lands, and, in one case we were urged to find, at once, a foreign girl for domestic service. . . . No pains have been spared properly to answer inquirers. . . . There is also a miscellaneous correspondence, properly coming to us, financial, commercial, and ecclesiastical, which has the careful attention of the office.[21]

This does not mean that the wealthy American missionary force allied with nineteenth-century commercial interests did not suffer loss, endure hardship or experience fruitfulness.[22] Nor is it to suggest that missionary operations were a front for commercial businesses. It simply illustrates that

Protestant mission began to experience the side effects of the commercial world it came from. Namely, that an entanglement with commercial interests obscures Christian mission. There are ways the Korean church and mission structures have repeated the commercially colonizing mistakes of their American parents.

International business depends on obtaining capital through the mobilization of investors who are interested in gaining profit from foreign markets. Protestant missions adopted a similar method of funding. Therefore, so long as the middle and upper classes are onboard, those with access to these funders can find financial support. One reason there are so many white, individually supported Christian workers (I'm one of them) is because we can more easily afford to buy our way into mission with help from our friends, not necessarily because we are more qualified than everyone else. Many of my highly qualified Majority World friends, and some of my Western friends who didn't grow up in the middle class, simply do not have the kind of connections required to pull together the $50,000 to $100,000 price tag of yearly financial support.

Take Nothing for Your Journey: The First Missionaries

When Jesus sent out his disciples in Luke 9–10, he gave specific instructions regarding how they were to organize themselves. Particularly, they were not to take with them anything first-century people normally traveled with. "Take nothing for your journey," Jesus urged his disciples, "no staff, nor bag, nor bread, nor money—not even an extra tunic" (Luke 9:3). For first-century merchants this would be foolhardy advice, even hazardous. But the disciples were to be desperately dependent wayfarers, without the insulation of extra cash or the comforts of home—completely marooned were it not for the help of God and the people they had been sent to. The journey they undertook would be more than inconvenient; it would be dangerous. "Sheep among wolves" was how Jesus described it. Self-sufficiency was not an option. Their mission was to look for people of peace and to rely on their hospitality. "Remain in the same house, eating and drinking whatever they provide," he said to them. "Do not move about from house to house" (Luke 10:7). They were to plant themselves in local soil and survive off the local food and customs. In a sense, they were not to be owned and run by investors as in a corporate model, but they were to be locally owned and operated.

Jesus paints a picture of woefully under-resourced disciples (at least in the worldly sense), living at the mercy of locals, healing those who were sick, proclaiming peace and letting their hosts know that God's kingdom was near. These disciples were peripatetic—regularly on the move and not settling down for long in any single location. Some people would welcome the message, and others would reject these Christ-followers and the news they carried, even going so far as to run them out of town.

Self-sufficiency was not an option. Their mission was to look for people of peace and to rely on their hospitality.

From what I can gather from the acts of the early "sent ones," this pattern was repeated, at least for those who itinerated for the express purpose of teaching the nations to obey all that Jesus had commanded. There were also those involuntary missionaries who, because of persecution, famine or other forces, planted themselves permanently among a people not their own and became "locals." Regardless, the earliest expression of mission was accomplished by loosely structured and minimally financed traveling wayfarers, as well as through the migration of Christians on the run from persecution. Both sorts of missionaries were significantly woven into local cultures and supported by local economies.

For much of the first several centuries of the church, Christian migrants and missionary bands, making their way with few resources, prevailed as the missionary model. For more than a millennia and a half, virtually all Christian "sent ones" lived within the communities they had traveled to, eating their food, living in their homes and facing the joys or challenges that their neighbors faced without any special insulation. They were often sent by small groups of fellow believers with enough resources to get them where they needed to go, but sometimes not much more. They had to make their way picking up work where they could and living without the comforts of home. While not universal, this was the modus operandi of Christian missionaries for hundreds of years. As Catholic missionary ventures became flush with cash and embedded themselves in colonial efforts, and as European and American Protestant missionary societies patterned themselves after the for-profit trade organizations and created missionary compounds, we witnessed a departure from the historic form of locally owned and operated mission to commercially styled corporate mission.

DEPARTING FROM THE CORPORATE MODEL

The organization I work for, InterVarsity Christian Fellowship, has largely followed the Protestant for-profit business paradigm. Like many of the Protestant organizations born in the World War II era, we were staffed in our early days by veterans who had been given new eyes to see the big and tragic world we live in. They were inspired to make a difference and sought out those who had been successful in business to chair their boards and help organize and govern their fledgling ministries. In those days a handful of poorly paid staff crisscrossed the country while students ran the ministry on the ground. But as we grew, the business model became more prominent in how we operated. Today, if you walked into the national office where I work, you would find it indistinguishable from most corporate business headquarters. In fact, before we moved to our current location, the building I work in served as Rayovac battery headquarters. I doubt the office looks very much different than it did when it housed the multibillion-dollar battery corporation.

Of course, there is nothing wrong, per se, with an office of one hundred people working in separate cubicles. It's that the corporate package often comes with liabilities that do not get scrutinized. What are the intangible costs of individualized cubicles? What about policies that dictate who gets a walled office and who doesn't? How might a strict division of labor separate office workers from field realities? Too often the corporate model we adopt, along with its policies and hierarchies, comes with assumptions that are not adequately debated. These forms end up creating forms of elitism, fuel greater disconnection from realities on the field, and bend toward bureaucracy.

Staff who join InterVarsity are employees and share much of the contractual arrangements common to all corporate employer-employee settings. Like nearly all Protestant missions, InterVarsity staff must raise personal support to help cover the cost of doing ministry, something like $40,000 per year for the twenty-two-year-old, first-year, single campus minister. This entrance requirement automatically leaves at the front door those who do not have relationships with middle-class people and churches that are accustomed to supporting missionaries in this way.

Part of our shape is determined by the fact that we have chosen to give our donors the ability to take a deduction on their income by registering as a 501c3 organization. Like the official charities in many countries, this gives the government a fair degree of authority to dictate how we use our money—mostly insuring we have some helpful accountability structures surrounding us, but sometimes defining what they deem a "bona-fide business purpose" to our ministry. Unlike a Catholic order, for instance, where the missionaries are as much the mission field as the mission they are engaged in, we cannot use resources exclusively for the spiritual development of our staff unless there is a clear "business" purpose. Training staff to do a job—we can do that. But deepening the spiritual journey of a staff is a tricky expenditure to justify to the IRS because there is not a straight line from the cost of a spiritual retreat to a bona-fide ministry outcome. In essence, all money must be traced to a tangible ministry "product" consistent with our stated purpose. Advancing our staff's spiritual maturity does not easily qualify.

There are ways, however, in which InterVarsity's practices depart from the standard business model history has saddled us with. Practices that I

believe must become increasingly widespread if we are to break free of the
Christian-Industrial Complex. For instance, 1 percent of all our incoming
funds are redistributed to ethnic minority staff. These funds are adminis-
tered by leaders in our various ethnic minority communities in ways that
make most sense within those communities. This practice becomes a
bridge between corporation and local ownership. Additionally, numbers
of our white staff regularly introduce their nonwhite colleagues to their
donors, challenging those donors to contribute to their colleagues' needs.
In some places InterVarsity is working to craft reasonable part-time job
descriptions so that it is possible for staff to be bivocational. And recently
staff have been trained to solicit the practical involvement and expertise of
local friends, not just their money, to advance the mission. This redefi-
nition of our relationship with men and women who were formerly simply
donors builds a volunteer corps that ends up saving us money and relieving
the loads our staff carry.

Six-month sabbaticals don't make much sense in the for-profit world,
but InterVarsity enjoys a generous sabbatical policy. Even some of our administrative workers have been able to take advantage of the sabbatical
policy. Finally, local contextualization is highly valued within InterVarsity.
What works at Duke University is not expected to work at Madison Area
Technical College. Cookie-cutter ministry is out, and grassroots ministry
is in. These are aspects of our culture helping InterVarsity to explore ministry outside the corporate box.

THE LOCAL FACE OF STUDENT MINISTRY IN THE MAJORITY WORLD

Our value of seeking indigenous expression of ministry and our attempt
to make serving on staff accessible to poorer or less-connected people is
located deep in our organizational genetic code. In 1947 leaders from ten
countries gathered to forge a kind of United Nations of evangelical university student ministries. InterVarsity was one of those ten. The largest
ministry at that time belonged to the Chinese student movement. The

International Fellowship of Evangelical Students (IFES) has been fiercely committed to a vision of Christian student ministry that is locally owned and operated. Confronting the abuses of Christianity's colonial past, the IFES has refused to create a leadership pyramid where authority resides in the West and is headed by a CEO-style president. A general secretary guides the fellowship with virtually no direct authority over the field. This person is aided with the help of regional secretaries, who govern by influence and relationship rather than fiat and line management. These men and women have no power to fire or hire those leading student ministries in the countries they advise. The current general secretary, Dr. Daniel Bourdanné, is from Chad, his predecessors were from Australia, Singapore and Wales. The IFES has always held a high value on low structure, indigenous leadership, relational authority, and the responsibility of students and recent graduates to run the ministry on the ground.

Deep in the DNA of the IFES is also a pioneering spirit that calls rich and poor movements alike to send out missionaries. Brazilians pioneering in Angola, Sudanese going to the Middle East, and Koreans in Mongolia: this is the norm within the Fellowship. This organizational vision, relatively unencumbered by a corporate-styled institution, was embedded from the beginning. Former general secretary Lindsay Brown claims that this locally owned and operated version of mission "has drawn students into cross-cultural mission with no formal theological training and without needing to learn the English language. Pioneers have come from some of the poorest countries in the world."[23]

This lean structure allows for each movement to send mostly young people into university settings around the world with no "staff, nor bag, nor bread, nor money—not even an extra tunic," just as Jesus did. Structures requiring heavy, centralized authority and relying on a supervisory chain of command that ends in an American or British hub often require a great deal of money to operate, especially if the organization is staff heavy and spread geographically. But when student ministry is conducted mostly by students and recent graduates at a local level, quite a bit can get done for very little.

In 1975, five recent graduates from the student movement in the Philippines decided to band together and pioneer student ministry in the southern part of the country.

The plan was to find jobs and give their free time to foster the work. They had gone with no promise of employment, and it took almost three months before they all found work. . . . With a secular job, a graduate does not have much time to spare for student ministry—at most twenty hours per week. But a team of three or four graduates could pool resources and work more strategically with the students. Team members received minimal supervision and had to depend on each other.[24]

Allowing a ministry to be conducted by a community of "unschooled and ordinary" people, carried along by a passion and vision for Christ and his kingdom, working together in small teams or living at the level of (and often with) the people to whom they have come, is not the story that gets central billing in the Protestant press. The colonial model crafted by a corporate ethic has left too deep an impression in Protestant mission. Few Protestant mission organizations have ventured very far from the paradigm of middle- to upper-class board members from business backgrounds guiding the mission agency with for-profit sensibilities and sending mostly middle-class, formally educated white missionaries to live in microcosms of their Western nations.

> **Allowing a ministry to be conducted by a community of "unschooled and ordinary" people . . . is not the story that gets central billing in the Protestant press.**

FREEING LOCAL OWNERS FROM CORPORATE HIERARCHIES

How might Protestant churches, mission agencies and parachurch ministries free themselves from the slavery to the corporate model we have been handed? There is no panacea, but there may be some modest steps we can take to explore other models.

Reexamining our boards. There may be wisdom in including on our boards those who have business backgrounds. These men and women often come with a good sense about how to get things done and how to manage resources strategically. However, to allow the commercial sector to dominate the highest level of our ministries is unwise. Boards should be comprised of a diversity of people from many walks of life, including many of those whom a ministry is seeking to serve. For a geographically spread ministry it may be wise to create a network of local boards made up of people in the community being served. I would also suggest organizations move away from the corporate model of boards of directors and adopt more ecclesiastical models of elders or spiritual advisors, allowing decision making to occur at more local levels of the fellowship among those who are on the ground.

The bivocational option. This is standard fare for ethnic minority urban church pastors, but relatively unaccommodated and only marginally tolerated in the white parachurch ministry world. A more aggressive approach to defining ministry positions for bivocational ministers without burning them out could open the door for many. It also embeds ministers in local institutions, connecting them more personally to the economies, services and cultures of a local community. How might Protestant organizations work with a variety of employment situations? Are there best practices from those who have tried and failed or tried and succeeded from which we can learn? Perhaps this is a better place for business professionals to partner with ministries rather than at the helm of ministry decision making?

Creative in-kind giving. Christian organizations might focus more energy on calling local partners who may not be able to give money but who could help reduce living expenses of our ministers in their communities. Housing and transportation can be significant costs that might be reduced through creative, in-kind gifts. One ministry I know is in partnership with a local restaurant owner. The restaurant provides the local missionaries one free meal per day and enjoys their fellowship in his establishment. Like the graduates in the Philippines who pooled their resources in order to pioneer student ministry, some intentional communities may be able to collectively free up time for some members to conduct ministry.

These suggestions may not be practical in all ministry situations, but they represent a challenge to our imprisoned imaginations. We must recognize the challenges that have been passed down to us through our historic marriage to the commercial corporation. We must open our eyes to the ways in which this model can obscure mission. And we must seek to move toward leaner and more local expression of service.

As we go deeper into exploring the heart of our Christian-Industrial Complex, we must turn our attention to the central place that money occupies in our organizations and churches. If we hope to steer away from a commercial business model inspired by the capitalist corporation, we will need to reframe our relationship to money.

3

FROM PROFITS TO PROPHETS

Like much of sub-Saharan Africa, Malawi struggles to establish a basic economy to support its population. Eighty percent of Malawians are rural subsistence farmers, and when the demands of population outstrip agricultural productivity, everyone suffers. For decades now farmers have been slashing and burning in order to obtain more agricultural soil. What was once a heavily forested country is becoming dangerously barren.

On a recent visit, the challenges of this sputtering economy were brought home to me by two contrasting images. One consisted of the disappearing natural resources. Even the land surrounding the capital city, Lilongwe, has been stripped bare. I remember looking out on what was once verdant foliage only to encounter miles and miles of tree stumps. In the desperate search for arable soil and wood fuel, people have removed acres of woodland, accelerating erosion and washing topsoil into Lake Malawi, wreaking havoc on the marine life. Turning my gaze to the roadways running alongside the forest of stumps was another vision of poverty, the symbols of the well-supplied economic development industry in Malawi. Interspersed with rusted and rickety forms of public transportation were what seemed to be innumerable shiny, new SUVs emblazoned with the logo of a nonprofit development agency. These vehicles were buzzing to and from the only buildings in Lilongwe that were more than a few stories tall—the massive shrines to economic development that stand in shining contrast to the deforested landscape. In my short and admittedly limited view, the only development that appeared to be going on in Malawi was the development of the economic development complex.

Why do most of us act as if large infusions of cash are the solution to the pernicious problems of our world? Where did we get the conviction that if we just had a bit more money we could begin a new poverty alleviation program or begin a needed mission?

As Protestantism grew up under the tutelage of the capitalist ethic, the critical role played by money in commercial enterprises was impressed upon it, and by extension was passed along to the nonprofit institutions that emerged from the church. One of the founders of the Social Gospel movement in the late 1800s, Josiah Strong, preached that money was the key ingredient to ushering the kingdom of God to earth.

> Money is power in the concrete. It commands learning, skill, experience, wisdom, talent, influence, numbers. It represents the school, the college, the church, the printing press and all evangelizing machinery. It confers on the wise man a sort of omnipresence. By means of it, the same man may, at the same moment, be founding an academy among the Mormons, teaching the New Mexicans, building a home missionary church in Dakota, translating the Scriptures in Africa, preaching the gospel in China, and uttering the precepts of ten thousand Bibles in India. It is the modern miracle worker; it has a wonderful multiplying and transforming power.[1]

In stark contrast to missional groups like the Franciscans or the Waldensians (a proto-Protestant movement), both of which shunned the pursuit of wealth, money has become king in the Christian-Industrial Complex. It is seen as the fuel to animate the social and religious aspects of Christian expansion. Since wealth was perceived as a necessary ingredient to expand ministry, industrial church complexes began to crop up in the late nineteenth and early twentieth centuries in America's cities. These well-endowed religious conglomerates were labeled "institutional churches."

Because they were heavily programmatic operations, institutional churches required both larger physical plants and larger staffs to operate. It was in these churches that the use of the multiple seminary-trained clergy and other professionals quickly grew. A neighborhood or rural church might, it if were lucky, have a full-time minister and a part-time care-taker. An institutional church, on the other hand, might have many full-time individuals detailed to teaching, working with youths, visiting with the elderly, directing social service work, preparing and serving meals, and keeping the building clean and open, not to mention the traditional task of preaching and the gargantuan task of administering a complex program. Not only with their retinues of many paid servants, but even in their appearance and furnishings, many of the institutional churches resembled nothing so much as the homes of wealthy Victorian era families.[2]

Like the megachurches of today, churches then benefited by their ability to expand staffing and ministry reach. But at a certain point the institution is no longer a vehicle to take us to a destination; it is the destination. Social and relational distance between ministers and those ministered to increases. Maintaining the ministry complex becomes an end in itself and requires energy that lighter and nimbler churches do not need. The focus of English and American mission at the turn of the twentieth moved to funding the machinery that undergirded the mission. Operations had become more and more elaborate and resource hungry. Like the trade companies they were patterned after, English and American missionary societies and institutional church boards were chaired primarily by the investors who funded them, and their finance-oriented worldview influenced how they believed the mission should operate. Rather than producing new, smaller, more localized churches or missionary bands as they grew, the tendency was to consolidate money and power and to build monoliths. And so intimacy is sacrificed on the altar of efficiency, more becomes confused with better, and talented local leaders are lured away from smaller operations because of the clout that comes with working for an organization that commands popularity, possessions and pizzazz. The money-centric view of ministry has come with other downsides as well.

THE PROSPERITY GOSPEL HEADWATERS

While flying home from Mexico City I sat next to a Nigerian Christian gentleman named Legborsi, who leads a Nigerian human rights organization. We fell into a discussion about the rise of prosperity teaching in African churches. The prosperity gospel teaches that each believer is entitled to health and wealth if they have sufficient faith. Every Christian is meant to be rich and strong according to the prosperity gospel. I wondered whether the mingling of Protestantism with corporate-styled capitalism had influenced this since it has been less present in Catholic and Eastern Orthodox theology.

"Where do you think the prosperity gospel comes from?" I asked my seatmate.

"From the US," Legborsi said without the slightest hesitation. He continued, "I have seen African pastors who did not embrace this teaching attend theological training in the US and return with an obsession on health and wealth."

I asked Legborsi if he thought this was due to observing the lives of American Christians or whether it was the explicit teaching of American seminaries. I could hardly abide that there were Protestant seminaries worth their salt which actively taught prosperity theology.

"I cannot say," he told me honestly, "all I know is they come back from America with a love for money and telling congregants they should be wealthy. American-trained African pastors teach people to hold their gifts up in the air for all to see, and one pastor tells his congregation if they can only give coins then do not bother coming to church!"

I was curious about this anecdotal evidence that the origins of prosperity theology come from the United States, so the following day I asked a Zimbabwean Christian I had just met the same question: "Where does health and wealth teaching in Africa originate?" My friend smiled easily, "From America, of course."

It should not surprise me that the American corporate form of Protestantism should be the fountainhead of prosperity teaching. The relationship between money and faith is described by some American Christians in the language of a business transaction. One expression of this theology says that God is under a contractual obligation to financially bless us when we give money to Christian ministries. Oral Roberts, one of the early prosperity teachers, claimed that God would return to the donor seven times the amount of their gift from unexpected sources. He even went so far as to offer a money-back guarantee if a donor giving $100 to his ministry did not receive that amount back from an unexpected source within one year.[3] For the majority of Christians in the world who are poor, this sounds like good news, and like all good tapestries of deceit, there are threads of truth woven in.

Poverty, hardship and suffering are by and large not part of the Protestant American construct of the Christian faith, and so our theology around these topics is weak and sickly. As Christian leaders from around the world come to visit believers in the United States, they see a lifestyle of material gratification, lavish churches and ministry complexes, and a posture which assumes that following Jesus should be a materially comfortable journey. The truth is that God does promise divine presence in the midst of hardship ("When you pass through the waters, I will be with you" [Isaiah 43:2]) and God does long for shalom (material, spiritual and relational) within the community of the faithful. I believe that God hates poverty, sickness and oppression, and that the "kingdom of God and his righteousness," which Christ calls us to seek (Matthew 6:33), should be one of abundance. But the highly privatized aberration of this vision does not line up with Scripture. We presume large amounts of wealth should be individually controlled and enjoyed. The American Dream of a large home, two cars and loads of disposable income is the syncretized American expression of God's kingdom on earth.

Missionaries from Outside the Middle-Class Kingdom

A large number of the early English and American missionaries came from relatively well-to-do homes who enjoyed the individualized perspective of wealth and possessions. That is to say, many of the American and European Protestant missionaries of the nineteenth and twentieth centuries were raised with a worldview that emerged from an expanding consumer, capitalist economy, and this provided a lens through which they viewed the mission. By and large Protestant missionaries of this period were well-to-do men and women sent by societies run by business leaders via missionary organizations founded on a corporate business model. They could hardly do differently than to pass their understanding of Christian mission through the for-profit prism.

The issue of finances was not a central feature of conducting Christian mission until the modern Protestant mission era. Mission was not dependent on a large middle class, and missionaries from poor communities in the Global South today somehow have managed to mobilize themselves without large infusions of cash. They might have to live with friends and relatives on the mission field for little or no cost, or they might work on the side like George Leile. Life and spirituality and work and mission are hopelessly mixed together, and finance plays a minor role.

"I will never be the same again because of Smokey Mountain." So says my Filipino friend Joshua Palma.[4] He grew up among the rural poor. In his twenties Joshua sojourned to the metropolis of Manila in order to seek his fortune. Like so many migrating from the countryside, Joshua found himself living on a stinking mountain of garbage with twenty thousand others, mostly dumpsite scavengers. "Smokey Mountain really smelled strong in those days; smoke incensed the whole place day in and day out. And where wind blew the smoke elsewhere, flies swarmed." Joshua grew up in the Baptist tradition and got involved with a church near the Smokey Mountain dumpsite. While playing guitar at an outreach for the children of Smokey Mountain, Joshua became both encouraged and puzzled by a

Baptist pastor and his wife who deeply loved the residents of Smokey Mountain. "I witnessed how passionate they were in raising the conscience of the community against the top-down development project designed by people in power. I realized that God wants to strip from us all of our brilliant religious garb and allow us to come face to face with our utter helplessness." Soon Joshua became involved with a few missionaries from New Zealand and Switzerland who had moved into the slums in order to catalyze change from the bottom up.

One of the things you learn living, loving and serving alongside the poor is that your initial assessment of what the kingdom should look like may bear little resemblance to how your neighbors on the margins might envision the coming kingdom. Rather than another economic development project, Joshua and the mix of poor and nonpoor who had linked themselves together in mission began dreaming about a place of peace outside the dump, where the urban poor could encounter God. They allowed those among whom they lived to help define the mission. Lilok Farm came into being as a respite from the dumpsites and barrios of Manila. It offers a place to decompress from the challenges of urban poverty, to ask questions about the spiritual journey, to engage the Bible through drama and to soak in the natural beauty of the area. In a megacity that is not very environmentally friendly, Lilok Farm is an Eden-like wonder, complete with tropical foliage, clean air and dry composting toilets. It is powered by solar energy, and much of it has been built with the sweat equity of volunteers.

With fairly modest support from outside the community, Lilok Farm has become something of an oasis for the poor. It is a dedicated space. Dedicated less to preaching to the poor—they get plenty of that in the city—and more as a place for the poor to ask questions of God and to search for answers. Joshua calls it a place where "the freedom to interpret the Scriptures is given back to the poor and the unlearned." He goes on, "I remember one pastor asking us, 'Aren't you like the serpent in Eden when you encourage people to formulate questions rather than give them clear answers?' So I replied, 'What do you think?'"

Joshua's tongue-in-cheek humor may have been lost on the pastor, but he believes his poor neighbors must have the privilege of searching the Scriptures and encountering Christ just as the middle class and rich do. Since those with wealth and power can find in Scriptures reasons to justify their position, then the poor should be able to search those same Scriptures for answers to why they live in a veritable hell on earth.

> **His poor neighbors must have the privilege of searching the Scriptures and encountering Christ just as the middle class and rich do.**

Joshua manages to make ends meet through a variety of sources though he is a full-time minister. He works at Lilok four days per week for a small wage, which is generated by the people who use it. A few friends in the West occasionally give a small sum. And a friend from Joshua's days in Smokey Mountain allows him to use a slum residence free of charge. Joshua is content to live simply and to give himself to a life of serving his poor neighbors in the name of Christ.

In the midst of Western powerbrokers attempting to economically develop the urban poor, what slum residents preferred, when asked, was simply to have a quiet place where they could come and be at rest. Without much in the way of funding, Joshua and a few of his friends living in slum communities created a glimpse of the kingdom of God on earth. It wasn't a mission to generate more money among the poor, though that can be valuable. It wasn't about creating a school for children living in poverty, though I have seen much good come from such efforts. It was a matter of listening to their poor neighbors, allowing them to stimulate the missionary imagination and open up a space for people trapped in urban poverty to encounter Christ through quietness and questions.

HOW MONEY BECAME LORD

Scholars like R. H. Tawney (1880–1962) and Max Weber (1864–1920) have noted the drift of economics from the field of ethics. The creation and expansion of wealth is a presumed good. There is usually no attempt to question this assumption. Somewhere in the last five hundred years we have turned economic expansion into a simple equation divorced from its spiritual and societal implications.

In the aftermath of the Great Depression in the United States there was a desperate scramble to understand what contributes to economic decline or expansion at a national level. Simon Kuznets (1901–1985), a Jewish immigrant from what is now Belarus, integrated a series of economic formulas and published the results in 1937. His idea was to capture all economic production by individuals, companies and the government in a single fiscal measure that should rise in good times and fall in bad. Thus the Gross National Product (GNP, later redefined as the Gross Domestic Product) became the universal tool for measuring the health of nations. The assumption was that stimulating a country's economy was synonymous with growing the well-being of its residents and contributing to national health. Thus, the more wealth a nation produces, the better off its citizens.

Robert Kennedy said about the Gross National Product,

> It measures neither the health of our children, the quality of their education, nor the joy of their play. It measures neither the beauty of our poetry, nor the strength of our marriages. It pays no heed to the intelligence of our public debate, nor the integrity of our public officials. It measures neither our wisdom nor our learning, neither our wit, nor our courage, neither our compassion nor our devotion to country. It measures everything in short, except that which makes life worth living.[5]

While it may be true that some baseline of income and production can contribute to a robust community, the increase of national wealth without regard to other factors is a poor reflection of flourishing. Economic expansion may even be damaging. For instance, studies have suggested that even in expanding economies, if wealth is unequally distributed, then social problems such as obesity, teen pregnancy, mental illness, murder, incarcerations and other social ills will increase proportionately to income disparity.[6] Even Christian relief and development organizations have bought into the notion that we can purchase "development." The GNP is a poor indicator of the sort of health I believe we want to see in our societies, particularly where economic growth is fueled by a cycle of excessive consumption and thoughtless waste. Economist David Korten posits, "We might say that GNP, technically a measure of the rate at which money is flowing through the economy, might also be described as a measure of the rate at which we are turning resources into garbage."[7] Thus calibrating national health to economic growth apart from things like income disparity, environmental consequences or fanning the flames of materialism can actually accelerate various forms of national illness. Our attachment to economic expansion in our Christian missions and nonprofits is overdue for an examination.

By taking economics out of the school of the humanities, have we made the field less humane?

When did the multiplication of capital become a panacea so disconnected from any critical evaluation of other aspects of social health? In 1972 the University of Chicago dropped the requirement for a history of economics course for its graduate students in economics, believing that field of economics is a hard science and has little to do with the humanities.[8] Many others followed suit. This shift marked the conclusion of hundreds of years of economic theory drifting away from its relationship to philosophy, sociology and ethics, and becoming what it is today—simple, mathematical utilitarianism: the multiplication of wealth without regard to what is just and good and fair for all. We must ask: by taking economics out of the school of the humanities, have we made the field less humane? Have we given our governments, banks and corporations freedom to multiply and spend wealth without moral accountability because of a simplistic assumption that all economic expansion is good? I believe so, and I find that by their actions many churches, missions organizations and nonprofits have embraced the theory that injecting more money into their ministries will almost invariably advance God's kingdom.

Our minds are so accustomed to the association of financial increase with personal and social well-being that we are hardly able to acknowledge and define the corrosive possibilities of growing the wealth of governments, businesses and churches. It is telling that there are two main classifications of organizations in America: for-profit and nonprofit, as if making profit is the only way to understand how we can establish ourselves, the only lens through which we can imagine human collaboration.[9] An organization pursuing profit is a for-profit business. But if a group of people establish an enterprise focused on any number of other noble pursuits, it is identified not by what it is, but by what it is not.

Why should profit be the main genus by which we classify the vision and direction of our organizations? There is more to our coming together as image bearers of God than simply

> **There are two main classifications of organizations in America: for-profit and nonprofit, as if making profit is . . . the only lens through which we can imagine human collaboration.**

whether or not we are chasing after profit. The church needs to resume its prophetic role in living a different vision for this world and the human relationship to wealth. I lament that the church's role in challenging of the notion that money is lord has been largely abdicated. We have not only become silent as the ideology of financial increase takes up more and more real estate in our media and in our minds, but we have actually welcomed the preeminence of profit into our interpretation of the kingdom of God.

The church is designed to be an incubator for prophets, not profits.

JESUS AND THE GOLDEN CALF

Christians have a prophetic responsibility to live a life of contentment in an economy of consumption. "Nothing could be more economically destructive than an outbreak of widespread contentment," says Jonathan Bonk, research professor of mission studies at Boston University's Center for Global Christianity and Mission. Bonk has long challenged the levels of affluence and consumption enjoyed by Western Christians and missionaries. He has called for missionary training that addresses the shocking disparity of living standards between Western Christians and the Majority World residents they serve, and invites us to live more simply and become bridges to power for brothers and sisters living in poverty.[10]

In order to heal the church and its mission structures from the deception of economic growth as a central building block to God's kingdom, we must identify the destructive contours of wealth and possessions and distinguish them from those places where ownership and wealth are a normal and benign part of human existence. Jesus gave a great deal of attention to warning us about the dangers of accumulation, possessions and riches.

Luke 14:33 is an uncomfortable passage for anyone who wants to be a Christian living in a consumerist society. In it Jesus says, "None of you can become my disciple if you do not give up all your possessions." Surely Jesus simply means to say that we must be *willing* to give up all our possessions to become his disciple, not that we are actually meant to give them up. It's hyperbole, right? But what if living free from the grip of materialism was the chief sign of the followers of Jesus, even more indicative than a verbal proclamation of faith? What if the desire to own was infinitely corruptible, and living in defiance of that desire became proof of our discipleship to Christ?

Shopping has become a way of life. "Shop till you drop" is a humorous aphorism that we might overhear someone casually say after church and before heading to the mall. We joke about our shopping addictions openly with other followers of Jesus, but we don't generally joke about our addictions to drugs or alcohol. Nonetheless, most psychologists tell us shopaholism is a serious illness. In fact, in a consumer society more people suffer under an addiction to shopping than the number of people suffering under alcoholism and drug addiction combined.[11]

I believe that our love of wealth (whether residing in our banks or in our garages) is at least as dangerous to our souls as our pursuit of sex outside of marriage, despite the fact that the church is often conveniently silent about the former and fantastically concerned about the latter. I am not suggesting that we have to choose which sin we are more concerned about, but being equally careful about both things might be a good start. Examining Scripture, we can, as a matter of fact, draw a fairly strong set of connections between greed, idolatry and sexual infidelity. They seem to feed one another. Many of the Hebrew prophets in one breath condemned idolatry and the sex rituals associated with idols, and in the next decried tight-fistedness toward the poor and lavish extravagance toward self. Ezekiel claims that the true sin of Sodom, the city from which we get the sexually scintillating story of Sodom and Gomorrah, was not sexual malpractice but financial malpractice. "This was the guilt of your sister Sodom," says God through the voice of Ezekiel: "she and her daughters had pride, excess of food, and prosperous ease, but did not aid the poor and needy" (Ezekiel 16:49). The materialism of Sodom translated into sexual misconduct, because coveting, objectifying, owning and consuming becomes a harmful and idolatrous way of life. Our posture toward indulging material desires is easily translated into indulging our sexual desires. Desire-consume-repeat. This is the energy the world is powered by, and the people of God are to carefully avoid it.

Materialism turns the pursuit of possessions into a religion. Executive editor of *Christianity Today* and prolific author Andy Crouch suggests that "an idol is a cultural artifact that embodies a false claim about the world's ultimate meaning. . . . They all raise the question of the Creator God's truthfulness and goodness, subtly or directly suggesting that the Creator God is neither true nor good."[12] Possessions are often accumulated because we do not believe contentment is possible without them.

And those of us who chase money can do so because we do not really believe in a Creator who is cognizant of our circumstances and capable of providing. In ancient Israel idolatry was expressed in the iconic incident in Exodus 32, when God's people declared the golden calf to be their true liberator from Egyptian slavery. In consumer society the emphasis has been more on the gold than the calf, but the fact remains that for modern society the iconic symbol of our liberation is the almighty dollar. I find it either a brilliant warning or an amazing paradox that "In God We Trust" adorns US currency. It should be a prophetic challenge to us every time we make a purchase—do we trust God or money, because we cannot have it both ways. Even one of Israel's greatest kings, Solomon, who at the start of his reign was not interested in wealth (1 Kings 3:11-12), descended from the heights of faithful devotion to the depths of unrestrained idolatry by sliding down the slippery slope of materialism and accumulation. This involved, among other things, accumulating and consuming "objects" in the form of his wives and concubines (he had in excess of one thousand, according to 1 Kings 11:3). Solomon ended up possessed by his possessions. The love of capital and the stuff it buys became an idolatrous pitfall. St. Paul warned that the desire for wealth is a root sin, a radioactive core out of which many kinds of spiritually harmful practices and attitudes radiate (1 Timothy 6:10).

Christians often define the slippery slope in terms of sexual immorality, but according to Scripture, the slipperiest slope on earth is greed and the idolatry it inspires. "Don't be greedy, for a greedy person is an idolater, worshiping the things of this world" (Colossians 3:5 NLT).

Jesus warned against the corrupting power of wealth and possessions in the Gospels five times more than he addressed the issue of sex outside of marriage. I count seven passages in the Gospels where Jesus warns against sexual infidelity.[13] I believe these warnings to be appropriate and critical to our spiritual health. But Jesus' concern for his followers' spiritual health was most often and most clearly expressed when he warned them about their relationship with possessions and money. The love of money is infidelity toward God. You might say that Jesus was more concerned about how his disciples misused their coins than how they misused their loins. Fidelity to God and his kingdom is best measured in our affections for the material world.

The thirty-six passages where Jesus warns his followers about the spiritual toxicity of money and possessions are weighty, and each one deserves careful examination.[14] But the following are a handful of places where Jesus speaks

> **Jesus was more concerned about how his disciples misused their coins than how they misused their loins.**

about the dangers surrounding the love of money and possessions.

> Do not store up for yourselves treasures on earth, where moth and rust consume and where thieves break in and steal; but store up for yourselves treasures in heaven, where neither moth nor rust consumes and where thieves do not break in and steal. For where your treasure is, there your heart will be also. (Matthew 6:19-21)

> No one can serve two masters; for a slave will either hate the one and love the other, or be devoted to the one and despise the other. You cannot serve God and wealth. (Matthew 6:24)

> What will it profit them to gain the whole world and forfeit their life? (Mark 8:36)

> Jesus looked around and said to his disciples, "How hard it will be for those who have wealth to enter the kingdom of God!" And the disciples were perplexed at these words. But Jesus said to them again, "Children, how hard it is to enter the kingdom of God! It is easier for a camel to go through the eye of a needle than for someone who is rich to enter the kingdom of God." (Mark 10:23-25)

> He said to them, "Take care! Be on your guard against all kinds of greed; for one's life does not consist in the abundance of possessions." (Luke 12:15)

As a result of these teachings the early church exhibited extreme caution around wealth and those who possessed it. They worked diligently so that those who owned a great deal of money and possessions would not have their faith choked off by wealth's hypnotic lure, nor would the wealthy exercise undue influence over church leaders or the mission of God because of their wealth. It is true that wealthy Christian benefactors do not always use their wealth as license to dictate mission, though some do. More often it is the fear of losing a benefactor's contributions that shapes our decisions. It is this posture toward wealth and its sources that can confuse decision making.

HOW THE EARLY CHURCH GUARDED AGAINST GREED

In a letter written to the church at Corinth around A.D. 130, early church father Clement of Rome commended the Corinthian believers who had sold themselves into slavery so they could use the proceeds to buy the freedom of those in slavery. "We know that many among ourselves have delivered themselves to bondage, that they might ransom others. Many have sold themselves to slavery, and receiving the price paid for themselves have fed others."[15] Like George Leile, these believers were not only free of a love of material wealth and the pursuit of comfort, but they were unafraid to sell themselves into indentured servitude in order to buy freedom for others.

One ancient document, the *Didascalia Apostolorum*, written somewhere in the early part of the third century, is devoted to the practical outworking of the faith and the conduct of church leaders. It governed how the church and its leaders were to live and how they might interact with those possessing great wealth or no wealth at all.

> And let the bishop be also without respect of persons, and let him not defer to the rich nor favor them unduly; and let him not disregard or neglect the poor, nor be lifted up against them. And let him be scant and poor in his food and drink, that he may be able to be watchful in admonishing and correcting those who are undisciplined.[16]

The church leader was to be exemplary in conduct—this meant living in the way of Christ and the apostles, in simplicity and voluntary poverty—in order to show the way for the followers of Christ to live. Like God's vision for Israel's kings (Deuteronomy 17:14-20), church leaders were not to be rich or favor the rich. When a bishop saw a rich person enter the church, he was not to show any special regard. When a poor person or an elderly person entered, however, the bishop was to "with all thy heart, provide a place for them, even if thou have to sit upon the ground; that thou be not as one who respects the persons of men, but that thy ministry may be acceptable with God."[17]

This is not to suggest that purchasing things that beautify our lives or acquiring possessions that allow us to be hospitable are wicked quests. But in every way, the power of wealth and possessions to seduce early believers was to be held in check. The worship of God and the pursuit of his kingdom were not to be trumped by the pursuit of money, nor was money to become the North Star to guide the church in seeking first God's kingdom and its righteousness.

MISSIONARIES FROM THE BOTTOM BILLION

The International Mission Board of the Southern Baptists say that the average cost of an individual missionary is $4,250 per month.[18] The Evangelical Free Church in America places the cost of a missionary family in Germany at $10,338 per month.[19] When you remove ministry expenses and break out the actual monthly salary that these missionaries live on (roughly half of the monthly figures listed), we find it is not exorbitant, at least not by Western middle-class standards. I would guess that most Western missionaries live fairly modest lifestyles overseas. For me, the issue is not that Western missionaries are living extravagantly, it is that their entire salary and benefit package, all of their ministry expenses, some of their living expenses and their children's educational costs are packaged inside an overhead-laden business model that must be supplied largely by missionaries' connections to people of means. Western missionaries have come to expect employee-employer style contracts with agencies, which include these costs in the employment package. It is relatively rare to find Western mission organizations that take bivocational ministry seriously or who seek to minimize living costs through in-kind gifts like housing or transportation. When missionary service is relegated to those with access to $100,000 in yearly in support, we create a very select priesthood with access to the financial holy of holies, while masses of qualified kingdom servants stand in the outer courts.

The "bottom billion" refers to the one billion residents living in desperate poverty who must overcome seemingly insurmountable odds in order to stabilize the heart-wrenching tide of loss and suffering. Some of the countries in the bottom billion, countries like Nigeria, Zimbabwe and Ethiopia, are nonetheless sending out missionaries. Regarding the stunning number of Christian workers that impoverished Majority World communities are sending crossculturally, Paul Borthwick, professor of missions at Gordon College, says, "They might go as missionaries, but they run their own Internet cafes, repair cars, farm, do medical work or serve as veterinarians. . . . They go expecting hardship and the need to create sources of income for themselves."[20]

Majority World missionaries operate on a fraction of the budgets of Western missionaries. Their standard of living is not only lower, but their structures are lighter. They simply can't afford to run the monoliths we have created as our primary sending structures. This is not to suggest that Majority World structures and the cost of running them will not expand if economies in these countries expand. It is only to say that large, expensive structures are not necessary for effective mission. Perhaps there are even benefits to keeping our ministries small and light. Rather than fighting Goliath in Saul's armor, our Majority World sisters and brothers are picking up five smooth stones and a sling. Perhaps we need to learn something from them.

Philip and Beauty Ndoro were launched as missionaries to Mexico from their home country in Zimbabwe in early 2009, at the height of an economic meltdown. For the previous ten years the Zimbabwe government had been reassigning farming operations away from white landowners and handing them over to black farmers. It was an attempt to correct land injustices committed during the colonial period. It did not go well. The new farmers didn't have the experience necessary to run the farms as efficiently, and agricultural production plummeted. This eventually shoved an economy teetering on the brink of disaster over the edge. Inflation in Zimbabwe during this period exceeded 6 sextillion percent (that's six followed by 21 zeros). Prices were doubling every other day, unemployment reached 80 percent, and people were literally dying on the streets.[21] In this financially catastrophic atmosphere Philip and Beauty became certain of their calling as missionaries. The lack of access to money did not need to impede their pursuit of God's kingdom overseas.

Philip and Beauty Ndoro, Zimbabwean missionaries to Mexico, with their children. Photo: Heather Torres.

Procuring a visa proved an additional challenge. Zimbabwe did not have a Mexican embassy, so obtaining a visa required more than two years of triangulating between a friend in New York who bounced between the Mexican consulate and Zimbabwean embassy, and Philip making two trips to the nearest Mexican consulate in South Africa. With uncertain support, the Ndoros embarked on their journey, financed primarily through friends in Western countries. They and their two children arrived in Mexico and planted themselves among the desperately poor residents of Chimal-huacán, a slum community on the outskirts of Mexico City.

Living simply among poor neighbors is standard fare for the mission organization they serve in. Their team embraces a life of voluntary poverty in order to pursue transformation from the bottom up, even as they also intentionally involve friends from other strata of society. The challenges that weigh on their poor neighbors also weigh on them. Their vision is to pursue flourishing—flourishing in their own spiritual lives and among their neighbors, all the while living in some of the most grinding circum-stances of violence, crime, drug addiction and poverty. The vision of this team of Zimbabweans, Mexicans, Venezuelans, Swiss as well as black and white Americans is to "establish the city of God within the city of humans, bringing [the] future into the present."[22]

Jean-Luc and Shabrae Krieg are cofounders of Mosaico, a community that was helped along by Servant Partners, a relatively young American mission organization. They, along with Philip and Beauty, are spawning a collection of Christian fellowships, community-based organizations and businesses within their impoverished neighborhood. This fellowship of national development workers, foreign missionaries who choose a simple lifestyle and involuntarily poor neighbors has launched community health initiatives, emotional recovery groups and youth leadership programs, multiplying house churches and citizen groups that work to obtain basic constitutional rights for their community. It is less about "development" as it is about releasing the assets, energy and leadership already there. It is a holistic vision of Christian mission accomplished by men and women that hail from both within and outside the community, and it is rooted in an understanding of the multidimensional kingdom of God. The hinge on which this church-planting, holistic Christian mission turns is not fund-raising but rich and poor working together to become the kingdom they want to see on earth. As Luis Armenta, holistic ministries director of World Vision Mexico, told them recently: "We are interested in learning more about your intervention model because it is a model that is able to have a profound impact with relatively few financial resources."

Mission Without Money

Full-time professional Christian workers are an asset to the church. At least I hope so since I am one of them. But there is honor and strength in Christians who are intentional about extending God's kingdom through their choice of where to live and where to work quite apart from pursuing employment in a mission agency, parachurch ministry or nonprofit.

Nigel and Jessie Paul are among those carrying a vision for nonprofessional Christian workers who are employed outside the Christian-Industrial Complex, and growing numbers are taking notice of them and those like them. They are gifted networkers. Twelve hundred people from more than thirty nations attended their wedding. You may wonder if they are rock stars to garner such an impressive wedding crowd, but Nigel and Jessie are simply generous neighbors living in a crowded, multinational neighborhood with a heart to see others doing likewise.

The Pauls live in an East Toronto neighborhood in one of four, twenty-five-story apartment complexes. It is a mishmash of urban poor residents from around the globe. The smells of curries compete with the fragrance of spices from West Africa and East Asia in a potpourri of international palates. Prior to their marriage Nigel and Jesse lived in two flats with a handful of their friends, all of whom had relocated in order to love neighbors who had little choice but to live in urban poor settlements. After falling in love inside this dense urban community it seemed quite natural to invite their neighborhood to the wedding. Jessie confesses to facing some fears as she began planning. "We started thinking about this wedding, and my excitement turned into fear as I thought about gang members causing, I don't know, problems at our wedding." As Jessie turned to God for comfort, she was drawn to Jesus' words in Luke 14:

When you give a luncheon or a dinner, do not invite your friends or your brothers or your relatives or rich neighbors, in case they may invite you in return, and you would be repaid. But when you give a banquet, invite the poor, the crippled, the lame, and the blind. And you will be blessed, because they cannot repay you, for you will be repaid at the resurrection of the righteous. (Luke 14:12-14)

After overcoming numerous logistical hurdles and operating on an extremely tight budget for twelve hundred people (they pulled the entire wedding off for just $5,000 Canadian), Nigel and Jessie were married in what amounted to two separate outdoor ceremonies in a nearby open field so they could accommodate the throngs of neighbors who responded to their invitation.

Their wedding reception, conducted in an impoverished Toronto neighborhood, is par for the course with this unusual couple. As a young entrepreneur, Nigel Paul wanted to challenge followers of Jesus to move into poor, immigrant neighborhoods. It was a simple vision of inspiring people to embrace Jesus' invitation to love our neighbors as ourselves. Why not choose to love neighbors who were materially struggling and who knew little to nothing about Jesus? But to do that required challenging Christians who were living in middle-class, homogenous neighborhoods to move out of those enclaves and intentionally relocate into places where they would be surrounded by people whose religious, economic and ethnic roots would be very different. It was a call to intentional displacement with a view to seeing the kingdom of God established. To do this Nigel built a simple website and began to attract Canadians who were interested in urban relocation as a form of mission. Since it was a challenge meeting virtually with people, Nigel decided to call together for a weekend gathering all those interested in relocating to poor, immigrant neighborhoods. He was not quite prepared for the seven hundred who showed up, so after the first day hearing about the value of relocation, he asked only those who were serious about moving into the poorest and densest neighborhoods to come back the following day. One hundred twenty returned. From that crowd, seven clusters of people made practical plans to move into seven neighborhoods, each of which met a few simple criteria for density and poverty, and which held a majority of people who would likely have little to no exposure to Christ. The only requirements for the relocators were that they pray as a community once a week and that they love their neighbors as themselves.

The idea began to take hold. By the end of that year, 2009, the loose fellowship of teams had been dubbed "MoveIn" and had launched forty people in ten communities living in ten different neighborhoods. One year later that number had doubled to eighty people comprising fifteen teams in fifteen neighborhoods. With extremely little structure and fueled by people that had chosen to live in poor areas inhabited by people of other faiths, the movement has become something of a phenomenon. By September 2013 there were 240 people making up forty-seven communities who now reside in seventeen cities in three countries. In four short years, with virtually no cash flow, Nigel and Jessie Paul and their friends have hatched a significant Christian missionary movement that does not depend on individuals raising support.

The mission of God is not built on money. This is good news for those trapped outside the financial strongholds but who bear a calling into mission. We have allowed our organizations and churches to be shaped by the call of the profits rather than the call of the prophets. While the business world has done much to help the church grow in its management of limited resources (whether time, money or personnel), there are many ways in which the excessive focus on finances has obscured or even co-opted the spirit and mission of Christ.

When the Protestant church hitched its train to the London Missionary Society and the American Board of Commissioners for Foreign Mission, it set in motion an industrial

> We have allowed our organizations and churches to be shaped by the call of the profits rather than the call of the prophets.

complex that followed the corporate vision of a capitalist enterprise, requiring large infusions of venture capital in order to get a mission started
and needed ongoing donor investment to keep the machine running. This
translated into the need to build fundraising societies in the eighteenth
and nineteenth centuries and eventually birthed the individual, faith-
based funding model, whereby missionaries must tap privately held wealth
to fund their individual salaries and personal mission expenses. This is one
way to fund missions—it might even be a descent way for those of us living
in an affluent society—but it is not the only way to run a mission, and it
becomes nearly impossible for those who are not connected to enough
people of means in order to generate a living wage. People like Mauricio
Alvarez from Uruguay could never have entered Christian service though
such a model. Mauricio is the executive director of a consortium of Hispanic mission organizations known as COMINHA. He accepted a high-
level job with a heavy equipment company under the condition that he
would be free to spend one week per month in full-time ministry. His job
allows him to employ bivocational Hispanic believers all over the world,
and the Hispanic Christian community is being deployed to see God's
kingdom come in places where missionaries are not allowed.

FREEING THE PROPHETS FROM THE PROFITS

How might Christian organizations trapped in a money-centered model
of ministry open themselves to less resource-driven ways of doing things
and release gifted but less well-resourced ministers? Some of the suggestions at the end of the last chapter may work to help reduce our reliance
on money, but here are a few more.

Centrifuge versus magnet. We need to resist the temptation to allow
resources to become a magnet, amassing in a central location and becoming
unwieldy. Rather, we should seek to spin off nimbler structures that might
be loosely connected (or not). Some innovative churches have done this.
The Underground in Tampa, Florida, is one example. It is a growing network
of one hundred microchurches and small ministries, each of which operate

with very few resources (see tampaunderground.com). People often meet in homes and ministers are bivocational. It is a prophetic alternative to the large, centralized, corporate vision of Christianity.

When gifted leaders in our ministry have inspired ideas, the gravitational pull will be to incorporate these new outreaches into our existing structures. We become bloated, knowing only how to add and not how to multiply. Multiplicity happens when these emerging ideas and ministries can be released to operate on their own. The incubator is no place to live for very long. Allowing our churches and parachurches to spawn smaller, local ministries that may or may not choose to loosely affiliate will have the effect of pushing ministry and resources out to the margins rather than bunching them up in one place.

Redistribute. I realize that *redistribution* is a dirty word in some circles, but in a world where the bottom half owns less than 1 percent of global wealth and the top 10 percent owns 86 percent,[23] I do not see a way around the need for a radical redistribution. Some organizations (my own included) take a percentage of all donations and release this to our minority communities to bolster the funding of good ministers who simply lack access to the enclaves of wealth. Just how much redistribution is necessary and the mechanisms for redistribution will differ from ministry to ministry, but this should be an ongoing and open discussion, and the minority communities should be given the greater say in this process.

Turn the purse strings over to the excluded. In Acts 6 the excluded community (Greek speakers) received the short end of the stick when funds were distributed for their poor widows. The solution was that the apostles (the "included" Hebrew speakers) released control of the funds to those who were being overlooked. They chose a handful of godly leaders (all Greek names) to take charge of the common purse, trusting they would not commit reverse discrimination and shortchange the Hebrew-speaking widows (more on this in chapter 6). If our churches and ministries are to involve both poor and nonpoor, then we need to invite godly leaders with firsthand experience of poverty and exclusion to a spot at the financial policy table. Working alongside those who are familiar with how money operates in our world, we need those with access and those without to collaborate in making decisions about how money will flow in our fellowships. In the US, decisions about childcare, benefits and salary scales would likely be shaped very differently if the excluded were invited to co-create our systems.

We can no longer afford the price tag attached to the middle-class version of Protestant mission—particularly those living in the majority world or who are otherwise cut off from middle-class or wealthy donors. We need a different operating system, a new vision and a new way of thinking about the interplay between mission and money. It is time to embrace a version of God's mission that is not primarily fueled by money. Breaking out of our resource-driven forms of church and mission may allow us to break free of the gravitational pull that turns the gospel into a product, the church into a business and people into consumers.

FROM CONVERT TO COSMOS

From the Asok BTS station (Bangkok's Skytrain) it is a short walk to Soi Cowboy. In the summer heat the frigid Skytrain air conditioning bites my sweaty skin and a barrage of TV commercials blares from the screens mounted on the walls of the car, dangling in front of us products I have seen and some I haven't. I don't watch much TV in the United States, but I can't recall ever seeing skin-lightening commercials. Here, they are as plenteous as US automobile ads. Like ads for acne medication, it seems to imply that dark skin is a dermatological illness. Another reminder of how the world is bent toward the minority of light-skinned people who occupy the planet, and how we live under a torrent of appeals to spend so much on things that matter so little.

As the BTS vomits us out onto the platform at Asok, we are embraced by the humidity. For the first ten seconds it is actually welcome, but soon the air becomes a suffocating blanket. I am accompanied by a handful of university students participating in the Global Urban Trek. We are preparing to walk through one of three red-light districts catering to Westerners. After our briefing by Ivan and Kashmira, a couple who serve with Youth With A Mission and who live and serve alongside sex workers, the student's eyebrows are arched in trepidation and they look out on the world through gaping eyes. They are mostly quiet. One student, Andrew, pulls me aside. "This is the most real thing I have ever done," he confesses.

We pair up to walk the gauntlet of go-go bars on either side of the Soi,

and Ivan sends us out in intervals, like animals boarding the ark in antici-
pation of a mighty flood. We are told to look with the eyes of God, listen
to what he tells us and to pray. Although I do this prayerful immersion
every year, I am too overwhelmed by sensory input to hear God. Women
line either side of the passageway like cereal boxes in a grocery store aisle.
Music thumps, the street swarms with mostly older men from the West,
and lights pulse in hopes of outdoing the bar next door. It's enough to
trigger a seizure.

Outside one go-go bar I see something I haven't seen in the dozen or so
years I've been doing this. The women here are adorned with identical neck-
laces, and each necklace dangles a small black disc displaying a number. To
those shopping for a sexual encounter, these are not human beings made in
the image of God, full of intelligence and creativity and complexity. They
are not unbelievably imaginative creatures capable of wielding the authority
and intellect to build a bridge or transplant a kidney or maneuver a craft ten
thousand miles in space. These women are commodities, items for sale.
Their bodies can be ordered by number, just like an item on the Extra Value
Menu at McDonald's, so that one doesn't have to remember a name, doesn't
have to confront the reality that these are our sisters. It makes it easier to
exploit a nameless body for a few moments and then to discard it without
jeopardizing one's conscience. In fact, some of these men will pay more to
have their lawn mowed by the kid next door than to share one of the most
intimate human encounters with a woman on this street.

We return to the guest house to meet up with the others who have had
similar experiences in other red light districts. We are shell-shocked. Some
students ask hollowly, "What's wrong with me? I can't feel anything!"
Others weep in prayer. Still others are taken to dark places in their past—
to that moment of their own experience as the molester or the molested.

We live in a world where anything, even dignity, is for sale. Most of us
live under an assault of five thousand advertisements each day, five
thousand attempts to arouse our covetousness, inflaming our desire for
things belonging to our neighbor (to borrow the language of the Tenth

Commandment), whether our neighbor's house or our neighbor's spouse. Covetousness is humanity's Achilles' heel, and we are so easily enticed to desire objects or to objectify the thing we desire. It beckons us to see the world as a set of products to be accumulated or consumed. Anything can become a personal possession. Even profoundly spiritual matters can be reduced to a possession.

The Gospel as Product, the Church as Business and People as Consumers

The consumer worldview under which most of the world has operated for the past one hundred years has slowly been shaping our view of people and ideas. It has also shaped our view of church and of the gospel. For at least the first three hundred years of the Christian faith, and in parts of the world today, human beings were not, by and large, predisposed to perceive the world in materialistic terms. It is more likely the pre-capitalist and pre-enlightenment mind would view life on earth as a stage on which various authorities vied for our allegiance. An individual came into the church as though coming under a certain alignment of powers, pledging allegiance to a new king and entering into a new dominion. Indeed "Jesus is Lord" was a political declaration as much as it was a spiritual one, defying one's allegiance to Caesar as lord and planting oneself in the corner of an opposing regime to all other principalities vying for one's loyalty. Christianity was a dominion as much as it was a lifestyle and belief system. But all that has changed.

As the lords of political regimes have sold themselves to the lords of corporate regimes, the statement "Jesus is Lord" stands in direct opposition to the mantra "profit is lord" or "business is lord." The principalities of profit have come to rule our nations. In fact, of the one hundred largest economic entities in 2012, forty of them were corporations. Everything is a commodity that can be sold, and individuals along with corporations can own just about anything. Even "time" is up for sale as futures are bought and sold on our trading floors. In this new corporate age our brains have been rewired in how we understand the world and how it works. We have come to encounter Christianity much like we might encounter a product or service. Fifteen hundred years ago becoming a Christian might have been compared to experiencing a kind of regime change from one emperor to another. Today it is more like a business transaction.

Brad S. Gregory, professor of early modern European history at the University of Notre Dame, writes about the Protestant Reformation's unintentional contribution to the secularization of society, not the least of which included fueling capitalism and consumerism. Gregory reasons that the "institutionalized worldview" promoted by the Catholic Church governed moral conduct. This was shattered by the Reformation, allowing for highly individualized interpretations of morality. Like Weber, Gregory sees moralization of accumulating wealth arising from Calvinist and Puritan theology and fueling the freight train of consumerism. In his book *The Unintended Reformation* he suggests that Western society has become "a wall-to-wall commodification of everything, exempting neither religion, nor weddings, nor women's ova, nor men's sperm, nor the human body itself, in a milieu into which children are acculturated literally from infancy."[1] I would contend that the conformity of our churches into shop-like entities is part of this commodification. Black urban churches often didn't have the money to buy a church building, so they met in defunct stores. It was called a storefront church, and in many ways they defied the business model with bivocational pastors and adaptive spaces where people met to worship. Many Protestant churches today have moved away from the informal, abandoned storefront as a container for church and have built what I might call "store-hearted" churches. It is as if we are trying to re-create the consumer environment of a mall or coffee shop inside our churches in order to attract customers. Friends of mine who attend a megachurch brought their three-year-old daughter for the first time into a Starbucks. "Mommy, are we at church?" she asked. Our churches have so contextualized themselves to a consumer culture that we have danced dangerously close to syncretism with a paradigm of product and consumption. Speaking about the influence of consumerism on secular society, Gregory notes, "Practices once regarded as dangerous and immoral because detrimental to human flourishing and to the common good have in a dramatic reversal been redubbed the very means to human happiness and to the best sort of society."[2] We like to display our faith through consumerism. Purchasing religious paraphernalia—tee shirts, jewelry, bumper emblems—is as likely a way an American Christian might express their faith as serving people on the margins.

The Protestant church unintentionally accelerated a consumerist mindset rather than offering an alternative vision to the corporate model commanding our fidelity. Seeking first the kingdom of God ought to consume us; rather, we have turned the kingdom of God into a consumable.

We've attempted to press the gospel into product form—a privately owned salvific experience obtained through a business-like transaction. This is the modern Protestant equivalent of purchasing indulgences.[3] The good news has

> **Seeking first the kingdom of God ought to consume us; rather, we have turned the kingdom of God into a consumable.**

lost its cosmic meaning and has been truncated from the reconciliation of all things by the grace and governance of a good God to an individual purchase of fire insurance. We buy God's friendship at an individual level with the transaction of a sinner's prayer.

To be sure, Christ's righteousness in exchange for our sinfulness is an amazing offer. But when people steeped in a consumer culture present or receive such an offer, the temptation to privatize and commodify the transaction is nearly too much to bear. I come to "own" my salvation experience as I would an umbrella. On sunny days I tuck it away, going about my business. But when the "great and terrible day" comes, I will have it ready for my personal protection. A saving relationship with Christ becomes a personal object to be enjoyed by me alone. Any cosmic or communal understanding of Christ's redemptive work, any reorientation of reality or submission to a new order is subordinated to the private ownership of my salvation umbrella. Scot McKnight argues in *The King Jesus Gospel* that we have exchanged the gospel of the kingdom for the gospel of salvation. Christ's global, messianic role as part of the story of Israel is lost in our personal salvation experience. The gospel is reduced to a redeemed convert instead of a redeemed cosmos.[4]

If the good news is primarily about a private exchange, then it can be sold through persuasion, and our churches are simply distributers or stores marketing the product. My wife, Janine, recently encountered someone passing out brochures to get people to come to their church. "No thanks," my wife replied, "I'm already part of a church." "Well, why don't you take this brochure anyway," the woman responded, as if to say "you still might want to consider dropping out of your church and joining mine." This woman was advertising her church with the help of a slick brochure and a "don't take no for an answer" attitude. She had reduced herself to a salesperson and Janine to a customer. This person's hope was that Janine might "purchase" the gospel through the same outlet where she "buys" the gospel. Her "gospel outlet store" was superior to the church we attend. We even use the term *church shopping*, reducing the Christian community itself to a product in addition to the gospel it sells.

We see something of the businessfication of the faith in our language. Many churches and most nonprofits and mission agencies have succumbed to using the nomenclature and methods of the for-profit world. Churches have employees, mission agencies are run by CEOs, we "brand" our church or mission identity to distinguish ourselves from our competitors, eighteen- to twenty-two-year-olds become target markets, donors are invited to invest in our ministry, and the needy become our clients. We think that this dialectic of the business world somehow helps to clarify our mission, but I don't think this is true. I believe it clouds our vision. Semantics matter. We are shaped by the language we use. To use the language of commerce for God's kingdom is to commercialize it. If, for instance, Walmart insisted on calling their CEO "high priest," that would alter the way people perceived the role of CEO and how employees relate to him or her. Particularly if the CEO adopted clerical robes for attire. If the company referred to Walmart stores as temples, to sales transactions as acts of worship and to

To use the language of commerce for God's kingdom is to commercialize it.

Walmart employees as apostles, we would call Walmart a cult. But if we use the for-profit nomenclature and operating methods for our churches, we call it a church growth program.

CHOOSING A MISSION OVER A MORTGAGE

When the church is reduced to a business, rather than establishing organic communities of believers in a variety of diverse forms and contexts, success becomes the reproduction of buildings on each street corner and the multiplication of clergy. Quickly reproducing businesses have become the templates for our churches and nonprofits, and we mimic and implement whatever tactics work in hatching a business empire or hustling a product. Location, location, location works for business; let's then pay a premium to get prime real estate for our churches. Or build a great edifice (complete with Starbucks-like coffee shop), contract with a consultant, hire an attractive and charismatic preacher, build a great contemporary worship band, and you've leveraged the great wisdom of for-profit business to plant a church. But this sort of spiritless application of business smarts doesn't always translate well into God's cosmic kingdom mission. We end up churching a building rather than building a church.

American missions in the late 1920s went through a financial crisis. Giving to missions was plummeting and nobody quite knew why, so a study was undertaken to find out. The study revealed that American Protestant Christianity had gone on a building spree and had financed their structures with debt. Building churches became a bit of a craze; owning a building became an apparition of success. "In the Methodist Episcopal

Church alone, $4 million in interest was being paid each year out of receipts of roughly $100 million. Methodists were paying more interest to banks each year in the late 1920s than they were giving their Board of Foreign Missions."[5] The American congregation had moved out of the schoolhouse or town meeting hall and had constructed institutional churches as behemoths from which to run their Sunday gatherings and associated ministries. The church had chosen a mortgage over a mission.

This same mistake was made again at the turn of the twenty-first century in the United States. The lucrative mortgage rates of the mid-2000s lured many churches into an expansion craze. Now some churches that overreached in their building programs are in default, and money that might have been used to fund mission or care for the needs in their community is tied up in bankruptcy court.[6] It has only been in the last few centuries that our vision for church became bound up with the notion of owning property and constructing a building rather than gathering in both public and private spaces[7] to share a meal, teach each other, pray, sing and address each other's material, spiritual and emotional needs.

I do not think the chief mission of God has anything to do with building more or bigger churches and ministries. "We cannot imagine any Christianity worthy of the name existing without the elaborate machinery which we have invented," early-twentieth-century Anglican missionary to China, Roland Allen, once complained.[8]

> Our modern practice in founding a church is to begin by securing land and buildings in the place in which we wish to propagate the Gospel, to provide houses in which the missionary can live, and a church, or at least a room, fitted up with all the ornaments of a Western church, in which the missionary may conduct services, sometimes to open a school to which we supply the teachers. The larger the establishment and the more liberally it is supplied with every possible modern convenience, the better we think it suited to our purpose. . . . Hence the opening of a new mission station has

become primarily a financial operation, and we constantly hear our missionaries lament that they cannot open new stations where they are surely needed, because they have not the necessary funds to purchase and equip the barest missionary establishment.[9]

When Christianity impersonates the corporate world, we don't need God. We can accomplish our mission with more money, a building and a bit of ingenuity. But the mission of God has never been simply about building churches or filling pews. The church is not a franchise, and people are not targets to whom we sell Christ. The highly individualized salvation experience sold through skills of persuasion is a shadow of the all-encompassing power of the gospel. But these are the methods we often use to measure and celebrate our mission success. The number of gospel outlets and the number of people who frequent them dominate our annual reports (another manifestation of the for-profit paradigm). But these are not the best metrics with which to measure the glory of God and the "increase of his government and peace" (Isaiah 9:7 KJV). They are phantom indicators shaped by a consumer mindset (see chapter 8). We have "exchanged the glory of the immortal God for images resembling a mortal human being" (or, I might add, a mortal corporation) (Romans 1:23).

If the gravitational pull of the corporate mindset is to hustle the gospel as a product or to see people as markets and churches as simply buildings through which one may buy or sell spirituality, then what is an alternative perspective?

> **The church is not a franchise, and people are not targets to whom we sell Christ.**

THE ORIGINAL GREAT COMMISSION

The original Great Commission was for humans to rule as the vice regents over creation in communion with the Creator. Human beings, like nothing else in the seen and unseen universe, are fashioned in God's image.

The man and woman inherited God's ability to reason, to create and to govern with beauty and benevolence, and our mission has ever been the flourishing of God's dominion and revealing God's glory through our lives.

"Be fruitful and multiply, and fill the earth and subdue it; and have dominion over the fish of the sea and over the birds of the air and over every living thing that moves upon the earth" (Genesis 1:28). This was the very first directive to humanity. We possess the raw God material to energize a thriving planet. The original "mission," if we are stuck with this imperialistic word from our colonial past, was to manage ourselves and our world under God's authority and design. As Andy Crouch puts it in his book *Playing God: Redeeming the Gift of Power*, "These image bearers will become the kind of persons who can themselves say 'Let there be' and 'Let us make,' not just deputies and functionaries in a heavenly bureaucracy of command and control, but agents of creativity in a universe designed to create more and more power."[10] This is quite different from the concept of creation as an object for us to exploit, a planet to use solely for our own benefit. Rather, creation emerged from the unadulterated goodness of the Creator, and the humans, made of God stuff unlike anything else, were invited to animate its flourishing. "The image bearers do not exist for their own flourishing alone, but to bring the whole creation to its fulfillment."[11] We were to do this in intimate fellowship with God and through the agency of the divine imprint of our Maker. We were made to "walk with God in the garden in the cool of the day," working in fellowship to fill, subdue and have dominion.

The first part of this commission, "fill the earth," uses the Hebrew verb *mala*, which has beautifully figurative undercurrents coursing through it. The King James Version says, "replenish the earth," and elsewhere in the Hebrew Scriptures *mala* is translated "fulfill," "consecrate" or "satisfy." There is something more than simply procreating or populating the earth in this command. God fashioned us in the divine image to satisfy something lacking in creation. It is as if there is a human-shaped void in the universe that only men and women can fill. We quench a cosmic thirst like nothing else.

The middle command, "subdue the earth," seems perplexing. The Hebrew word for subdue here is *kabash*. In English we sometimes say "put the kibosh on it," meaning to veto or to prevent something. Some speculate this phrase has Yiddish roots, so perhaps it is related to kabash. *Subdue* implies resistance and struggle. "Subdue the earth" shows up here and there throughout the Hebrew Scriptures. The same words for both subdue (*kabash*), and earth, or land (*'erets*), are used to describe God driving out his enemies and bringing the land under the authority of his people (see Numbers 32:20-22; Joshua 18:1; Judges 3:30; 2 Samuel 8:11; 1 Chronicles 22:18). While I don't believe this is license to "lord it over" the land or even over God's enemies, there is something here that implies an invitation to make right something that is out of order. The word *kabash* is also used at least once to describe what God does to our sin. The prophet Micah says that God will subdue (*kabash*) Israel's iniquities (Micah 7:19).[12]

Exactly what was God's intention in commissioning humans to subdue the earth? What in pristine creation needed the kibosh put upon it? With wisdom beyond my understanding, an intelligent, occupying force had been allowed to co-exist with humanity, a rebel bent on stirring up insurgency and wreaking havoc. Walter Wink, in his trilogy *Naming the Powers, Unmasking the Powers* and *Engaging the Powers,* describes the "world domination system" (sometimes referred to in Scripture as simply "the world") as the collection of principalities and powers that oppose God and God's good creation. Could it be that one great commission of humanity is to colabor with God in the subjugation of evil? At least let us concede that after the fall there is power and divine commissioning to take dominion over our sinful tendencies. God told Cain before he murdered his brother Abel, "Sin is lurking at the door; its desire is for you, but you must master it" (Genesis 4:7).

The apostle John describes one of the chief purposes of Christ in a letter to the churches: "The Son of God was revealed for this purpose, to destroy the works of the devil" (1 John 3:8). The late missiologist Ralph Winter asserts that our mission is to join Christ in his evil-destroying mission: "If the Son of God appeared to destroy the works of the devil," Winter says, "then what are the Son of God's followers and joint heirs supposed to do to bring honor to His name?"[13] He proposed that our calling includes addressing every area where creation has run amok, including hatred and its effects, or deadly viruses decimating populations.

Why entrust fallible, weak humans with this fantastic assignment of subduing the earth? Why not angels? Or better yet, why shouldn't God subdue the earth without anyone's assistance? I believe it is because we are God's ambassadors (2 Corinthians 5:20), and we carry the imprint, the talent, the authority, the rights and the responsibilities that come with that role. In Psalm 8 we're told that God made us a little lower than *elohim*, which is translated in some versions, "He made us a little lower than God" (Psalm 8:5, NRSV, NLT, NASB). C. S. Lewis says in his sermon titled "The Weight of Glory," "the dullest and most uninteresting person you talk to may one day be a creature which, if you saw it now, you would be strongly tempted to worship, or else a horror and a corruption such as you now meet, if at all, only in a nightmare.... There are no *ordinary* people. You have never talked to a mere mortal."[14] In the commodification of humanity we have forgotten that men and women are not simply defiled objects to be rescued, restored and placed on a heavenly shelf. We are invested with power by our very design to oppose the enemies of life, the systems of oppression and the deterrents to flourishing. Humans have the raw materials to overcome the forces standing in the way of thriving and the capability to satisfy a world which is hungry for our generous and self-denying governorship.

I will deal with the question of humanity's fall in a moment. But to think that if our ability to subdue those things (even within ourselves) that defy God's good creation is part of our Creator's intent, then we have what it takes to subdue racism, materialism, poverty, cancer, AIDS, pollution, human trafficking and many other maladies that curse God and confound creation. "For we are God's masterpiece. He has created us anew in Christ Jesus, so we can do the good things he planned for us long ago" (Ephesians 2:10 NLT).

"Have dominion over" (*radah*) is translated elsewhere "rule over" or "have charge over." Interestingly, the primitive root here is "to tread down" or "subjugate," perhaps expanding on the previous command to subdue the earth. Energy is exerted in exercising dominion, and the best kind of dominion is the protection of the vulnerable against the powerful and confronting that which brings injury or destruction to the good and beautiful. Just a few chapters later a similar word is used when God tells Cain that he must "master" or "rule over" sin. Cain was urged by God to take dominion over the internal compulsion to commit evil. So even after the wayward human being had succumbed to temptation in the garden, we see God inviting us to take dominion over our own evil tendencies.

Most often, however, this term *radah* is used in the sense of governance or supervision, like in 1 Kings 5:16, where Solomon's thirty-three hundred foremen had "charge over" the laborers. In another place, masters were warned never to "rule over" their servants with harshness, but rather to fear God (Leviticus 25:43). It is also used prophetically about Christ in Psalm 72, where the king's son was to "have dominion from sea to sea" (Psalm 72:8), again not with a sense of exploitation or iron-fisted domination but with an eye to care for the needy:

> May he defend the cause of the poor of the people,
> > give deliverance to the needy,
> > and crush the oppressor. (Psalm 72:4)

God intended humans to be superintendents of creation, rulers who enforced the kind of "rules" that benefit the greater good, especially looking out for and protecting the vulnerable. Survival of the fittest is not such a great system for those that aren't fit. With humans in charge, possessed of God's DNA and endowed with God's authority, the predatory forces would not go unchecked. God's superintendents were to manage every living thing with the same grace, creativity, beauty and benevolence that God had used to create the universe—promoting the good and subjugating the forces that worked against a prospering cosmos.

So, what of the fall in Genesis 3? Has the command to replenish, subdue and rule been revoked because of human rebellion?

The Ongoing Work of Emancipation

The fall in Genesis 3 may have twisted the human ability to oversee the flourishing of creation, it may have introduced a tendency to leverage power for the benefit of the few, and it may have impaired our judgment. But the fall did not remove God's fundamental design. We did not become utterly different creatures, no longer bearing God's imprint. Therefore, since we still have the stuff of God in us, I do not see how the fall has revoked God's call to replenish, subdue and exercise godly dominion. After the fall we continue to see God's people acting as a conduit, charged to bring shalom to the nations.[15] This is expressed very early on in Genesis when God promises Abraham that "in you all the families of the earth shall be blessed" (Genesis 12:3), and through the prophet Jeremiah, where God says that if Israel would only forsake their idols and commit themselves to God with truth, justice and righteousness, "then you would be a blessing to the nations of the world, and all people would come and praise my name" (Jeremiah 4:2 NLT).

The divine yearning for global shalom to be released through human agents is expressed in numerous prophetic themes: light coming to the Gentiles, the blind receiving sight, laborers reaping the benefits of their labor, the oppressed being set free and the land yielding its produce. These promises were not pictured as God pushing aside corrupt human beings and acting alone, but usually involved some kind of divine-human dance.

> Is not this the fast that I choose:
>   to loose the bonds of injustice,
>   to undo the thongs of the yoke,
> to let the oppressed go free,
>   and to break every yoke?
> Is it not to share your bread with the hungry,
>   and bring the homeless poor into your house;

> when you see the naked, to cover them,
>   and not to hide yourself from your own kin?
> Then your light shall break forth like the dawn,
>   and your healing shall spring up quickly;
> your vindicator shall go before you,
>   the glory of the LORD shall be your rear guard. (Isaiah 58:6-8)

The invitation to replenish, subdue and govern appears to remain in some form throughout Scripture.

Those living in poverty, foreigners, widows and orphans figure prominently in God's instructions to defend, deliver and protect those who are vulnerable. The sabbatical laws were for replenishing the soil as much as they were a call for the restoration and replenishment of the workers. The forgiveness of debts and release of bonded laborers on an every-seven-year cycle, along with the Jubilee every forty-nine years, was an invitation to correct things that had become imbalanced. Harmony, restitution, reconciliation and liberation are themes running throughout Scripture, and God's people were expected to play a role as carriers of God's virus of shalom.

GOD'S REINTEGRATING CENTER OF THE UNIVERSE COMES TO EARTH

But the day God donned human flesh the cosmos encountered the ultimate vision of redemption. At that moment the heavens burst open with a celestial concert never performed before a human audience. Delivered free of charge, it inspired and terrified society's bottom rung, simple shepherds. "Glory to God in the highest heaven," they sang, "and on earth peace among those whom he favors!"

The cry of a newborn rang out from a peasant's feeding trough. "The reintegrating center of human and cosmic life" had arrived on the planet.[16] And in the advent of Christ on earth we find a liberator, coming in helplessness and drawing to himself a rabble he would invite to do even greater works than he accomplished. It was an invitation for his followers to take up the command to replenish, subdue and rule. But if we look to the redemptive work of Christ as our example, we must confess that it will come with sacrifice and suffering.

Jesus spoke to his disciples about the emancipating nature they were to have in the world. He used the metaphors of salt, light and leaven as pictures of the influence his followers were to possess on earth. For some Protestants this has almost exclusively been advertised as announcing the redemption of humanity from sin. But Christ's redeeming work reaches into and then beyond the restoration of fallen humanity to a holy God. For the Eastern Orthodox community the mission of God has always been about glory. "The restoration of the universe supplies an added dimension to God's mission," Orthodox historian James Stamoolis says. "God's mission is an overall plan that redeems human beings and renews and restores the physical creation to what God had intended it to be before he created it. In all this, the glory of God is revealed."[17]

Though the restoration of all things in the universe through Christ was complete and immediate, we do not yet see it (Hebrews 2:8). Perhaps it is akin to the Emancipation Proclamation, which was an executive order in the United States in 1863, long before the reality of equality occurred. At that very moment on January 1, 1863, it was law, it was true, it was binding—and we have spent more than 150 years trying to hammer it into reality. Emancipation from slavery has been established, but there is still the charge and responsibility to bring that binding truth into practical daily expression. We're now in the period of civil war and civil rights, meting out those things into an earthly manifestation.

Power (*exousia*) and authority (*dynamis*) are key words in the New Testament. They are used over one hundred times each. Often, power and authority are tied to Jesus: "They were all amazed and kept saying to one another, 'What kind of utterance is this? For with authority and power he commands the unclean spirits, and out they come!'" (Luke 4:36). These words refer to Jesus' jurisdiction and abilities. It is within Jesus' right to correct injustice, forgive sin, heal illness and deliver from death, and why not? "Thrones or dominions or rulers or powers—all things have been created through him and for him" (Colossians 1:16). Since Christ was a participant in the creation of the universe it should not surprise us that he has the power and authority to put to order misaligned things. What is curious is that several passages have Jesus conferring *exousia* and *dynamis* on his followers. In sending the Twelve and the Seventy, Jesus transferred to the disciples power and authority over evil, sickness and God's enemy (Luke 9:1; 10:17-18). In many parables the steward or tenant is a key figure. In them, a king or landowner has gone on a journey. In his absence, stewards or tenants have been given power and authority over the master's realm or property. Some of the stewards rebel and reject their responsibility, while others fulfill them. In the end the king or landlord returns and makes things right by judging the rebellious and rewarding the faithful.

The followers of Christ are invested with power and authority over things that need governance or even subjugation. We are more than heralds. Spinning the gospel as a product might have us simply introducing people to a deliverer who will remove the yoke of slavery and relieve the pain of carrying a burden. While this might be a beautiful role to play, it is only a shadow of our complete mission. The mission of the Creator is not only to bring the enslaved to the yoke breaker, it is to work alongside him to establish a kingdom where there are no more yokes. Jesus came to save, and *sozo*, the Greek word for "save," is also translated "heal" and "deliver." Christ's work is all-encompassing. "Indeed, God did not send the Son into the world to condemn the world, but in order that the world might be saved through him" (John 3:17).

Christ said that God had sent him to

> bring good news to the poor.
> He has sent me to proclaim release to the captives
> and recovery of sight to the blind,
> to let the oppressed go free,
> to proclaim the year of the Lord's favor. (Luke 4:18-19)

Those who call him Lord must share something of that mission with their Master. I am unsure whether we can overcome every mutation of harmful viruses, but I believe he has given us the authority and intelligence to conquer malaria. While the poor may always be with us, I believe he expects us to exercise dominion over the most pernicious forms of poverty. While there always will be oppressors and constant challenges to the environment, I believe we have the equipment to deal a serious blow to corruption, oppression and pollution. While it may not be possible to eradicate all forms of sexual misconduct, it should be possible to make nine-year-old sex workers a rarity. We have authority to address forms of mental illness. I believe we are charged to colabor with Christ in beating the implements of warfare into the implements of agriculture. We are called to participate in the dawning and flourishing of Christ's government where it does not exist. This mission cannot be packaged as a product. It cannot be reduced to a privatized exchange. It is not a mission of individual prosperity but of communal shalom. It is a cosmic mandate to work with the Savior in replenishing all things corrupted by brokenness and sin.

REPLENISHING SOUTHALL

The signs on the Southall train station, just a fifteen-minute ride from the Heathrow Airport, are in both English and Punjabi. Stepping out of the station and onto the street, I can see why. In some local schools, nearly 100 percent of the student body is nonwhite, the majority of which are from India's Punjab region. Southall boasts the largest Sikh temple outside of India. The streets are a parade of color—sidewalks are set ablaze by women wearing salwar kameezes dyed every pigment discernible to the naked eye and draped with the scarf-like duppetta, and men with colorful kurta pajamas and white turbans next to one another in fraternal fellowship, hand in hand or arms around each other. Even the air is colored with the smell of a hundred curries.

But Southall also has its challenges. Some Southall residents have turned their backyard garden sheds into illegal rental properties and leased them to the overwhelming tide of immigrant families that have washed ashore. "Sheds with beds" they have been dubbed. These parts of Southall are London's version of the squatter settlement. It is one of those places on our planet that possesses the strange and stunning mixture of vibrant community, desperate poverty, amazing food, appalling human trafficking, halting pollution and a few breathtaking sections where God's kingdom and righteousness have kissed earth.

The vicar of St. George's heard God's still, small voice one morning as he walked the family dog past an empty lot that had been turned into a dumping ground. Motorbikes had discovered in this dumpsite a creative obstacle course where ditches, burned-out cars, shopping carts and rubbish created a daunting challenge. "How do you think I feel about this place?" Reverend Dave Bookless felt God was asking him. Dave confessed that in that moment he had "a sense of God's pain at the way in which we had spoiled this place. . . . But I also sensed God's sustaining and renewing work in the fact that there was still stuff growing."[18]

This was God's call to Dave Bookless to replenish, subdue and govern one small, derelict corner of the earth. But it is not so simple to undertake the redemption of a dumping ground. Various people and forces laid claim to that derelict lot. It was owned by the London borough of Hillingdon, and some politicians saw this site as an opportunity for commercial development. Sports clubs were thinking about building a stadium on that spot. A Sikh school on the corner of the site had an interest in seeing it kept undeveloped, and the local wildlife trust had plans to do something with this rubbish patch. Contending for this abandoned property in the midst of so many differing interests was a challenge for this Christ-follower simply trying take upon himself God's heart and passion for this portion of creation. Should Dave Bookless rally as much political clout as he could muster or raise more cash than the others to outbuy them? The believer's call to establish God's kingdom must balance serpent wisdom with dove innocence. Jesus told his followers, "You know that among the Gentiles those whom they recognize as their rulers lord it over them, and their great

ones are tyrants over them. But it is not so among you" (Mark 10:42-43).
Our methods must be infused with the grace and peace of the Creator.
Reverend Bookless and the believers who joined him had to learn a diplo-
matic dance. They worked with the various parties, stirring up a vision that
grew like a white blood cell count in a sick body. They stimulated a healthy
view of what a flourishing community needed, and confronted various
interests who might have preyed upon communal health. In the end, a lush,
country park came into being.

Minet Country Park is one of those places where the kingdom of
God and its righteousness have been striven for. A thriving park in the
middle of a poor, urban, immigrant community is a sign that God is
alive and working through believers. As Christians have contended for
this parcel of land, those who knew nothing of Jesus or had discounted
him have come to faith or have reconsidered what they assumed were
imbecilic followers of a mythical dead rabbi. The earth has been coaxed
back to life, people have come together to work in harmony, the poor
have begun to grow food, and believers have exercised power and authority for flourishing.

It's difficult to measure this kind of restorative mission. It cannot be
reduced to a number of converts or churches. Dave Bookless was released
by St. Georges from his post and, with the encouragement of the bishop
of London, started the UK chapter of a Christian environmental organization called A Rocha. Volunteers from many different faith backgrounds
have walked alongside these believers and participated in their Scripture
studies and prayers. Some non-Christian volunteers have become convinced that Jesus is the Christ; others have had their curiosity piqued and
their view of the Christian faith has been given substance. Kids at risk of
crime, sexual exploitation or drug use have taken part in programs at Minet
Country Park and encountered believers and churches. Young men in
trouble with the law have been assigned community service working with
A Rocha, some of whom contributed to the degradation of the park years
earlier when they used the park as a gang hangout.

Meanwhile, a handful of Christian men and women have moved into a poor neighborhood of Southall near the A Rocha UK offices. They are taking seriously the metaphor of leaven in the depressed places, and salt where flavor is needed, and light where the darkness is thick. With impact out of proportion to their size they form one of the communities of Servants, a mission that embraces a vision of Christian relocation into desperately poor urban communities. Near to them a young woman with International Teams works to address the trafficking in human flesh that preys on the life of the residents of Southall, providing care for women who have been sold into sex slavery by the pimp called Poverty. These believers from different organizations work together in Southall, supporting each other's programs as well as running their own. They are convinced of Christ's liberating supremacy and are working with him in the replenishing of all things—people, places, powers and the planet. They live simply and are supported by relatively lean organizational structures. They are integrated into the life of the community and enjoy each other's friendship, serving one another without worrying which of their organizations gets the credit. Many of them are bivocational. They are one vision of God's interconnected mission to replenish, subdue and govern. And a relatively poor, predominantly Sikh corner of London has not been sold a product or invited to a building or treated as a consumer; they have instead witnessed the coming of God's kingdom and righteousness.

Freeing the Gospel from Commercial Packaging

The intricacies of a mindset that has made the gospel a consumable or turned our churches and ministries into shops may be difficult to disentangle. A more robust understanding of the mission of Christ in the renewal and redemption of all things will help. But likely it will require us to make subtle and not-so-subtle changes to church and mission.

Changing nomenclature. It may seem benign, but reforming our corporate language will help. There are ways we can expunge the nomenclature of commercial business from our ecclesiastical and mission structures. There is nothing inherently evil in the terms *CEO, employee, brand, market, target audience* and so on. But I worry about the incursion of commercial attitudes behind these words. Lynn Green, a key leader with Youth With a Mission (YWAM), talks about the shift away from business language and toward the language of family. "Language shapes the way we think . . . and if you use terms like *director* and *CEO* to describe the way you function, then there is an implied obligation to function that way. . . . The first institution that God established was family." And so YWAM has undertaken reforming their language and their postures away from business terms and toward that of a family. Speaking about employment relationships, Lynn says, "Happily we have never had an employer-employee frame of mind. We have always been a family of people, each of whom trusts God for support; we each contribute as we are able toward a common purse from which we live in community."[19] A little creativity in our terms may yield helpful adjustments in our mindsets.

Broadening our view of mission. I do not think it wise to take on more than a very narrow aspect of collaborating with God in the mission of bringing all things under Christ. But our understanding of our piece in the larger picture is critical. If our piece is church planting or evangelism, then do so intelligently, with an admission of the limited part this occupies in the cosmic scheme of things. If it is in restoring the environment, ending child labor or creating wealth in a poor community, then recognize the infinitesimal sliver this represents in the grand mission of God. We need to be for one another and to celebrate the importance of each of our parts. Each person should be on a mission to eliminate the mastery of sin in their lives, bringing God's flourishing into their families and communities, and participating in some small way to the replenishing, subduing and governing of the world.

Participating with others. Acknowledging the limited role our church or ministry plays does not mean we cannot work in collaboration with others. There will be more to say in coming chapters on this, but suffice it to say for now that we should seek helpful partnerships. Those freeing men and women from exploitative industries should be in fellowship with those providing aftercare, health care and spiritual direction. No one ministry should attempt to do it all, but ought to work closely with other ministries doing parallel work. This, I believe, should at times include working alongside secular authorities as well as other faith expressions that are moving forward a mission of replenishing, subduing and governing. The imprint of God is in all creation, including every human person regardless of what they believe. We may long for our co-conspirators to understand the grace of God and the power of Christ to save, but it does not preclude our working together to bring flourishing.

As we unwrap the commercial packaging and paradigms binding our structures and our thinking, we not only move away from a product-oriented view of the gospel, but we can free ourselves from an overly individualistic perspective on life and spirituality. I believe that the corporate and the commercial worldview has aided and abetted a dangerous individualism. It is to the communal perspective that we now turn.

5

FROM SOLITARY TO SOLIDARITY

"We prefer to be called 'plain folk,'" David told me, but they seemed anything but plain. Life for this Old Order community seemed extravagant to me—extravagant in hospitality, extravagant in friendship and certainly extravagant in their enjoyment of food. Breakfast, lunch and dinner were massive affairs: freshly baked bread, raw milk straight from the cow, several hearty side dishes and some kind of main dish made of beef, pork or chicken from a creature that had been wandering about the farm not long prior.

A dairy farm requires rising early and a good bit of physical labor throughout the day. But work life conducted in the context of community is also fabulously social. One couple who spent a year living and working with an Old Order community estimated that at harvest time—a two-week part of the year when all hands were on deck and all rose early and went to bed late—the actual time in labor amounted to about forty-eight hours per week, and much of the rest of the days included a fair bit of socializing over breaks and meals.[1] I was impressed with how lavish the time spent around the table was for the Old Order Mennonites that my family and I spent time with. Each meal was at least an hour-long affair, sitting around the table chatting, laughing and hearing about life among the eighteen families who had formed a fellowship of "plain folk" about three hours from our home in Madison, Wisconsin.

For people I had never met before, David and Laura, along with their large family, opened wide their arms to us. David was eager to share about the journey of their community as I accompanied him in his farm work and errands, while Laura kept Janine and our youngest child, Laura, busy around the house. In many ways they were as conservative as they come theologically, though their commitment to nonviolence, their apprehension toward any kind of support of the political state and their activism in the raw-milk movement made them difficult to pigeonhole. But clearly this Christian community of "plain folk" had no lack of resources.

Their community of plenty is partly due to their deeply held value for sharing. Equipment, time, food and possessions are constantly flowing from one household to another. The lines of private ownership become blurred in community. This branch of Mennonites pays no health insurance, no car insurance, no life insurance and no home insurance. Their commitment to the faith and to one another is their insurance program, and this frees up a great deal of their wealth. As a farming community they are fairly well stocked with regard to their food needs, and what most of us might purchase, they manage to make themselves. The absence of TV and Internet keep them from a certain amount of inflammation of desire, and their commitment to material simplicity and plain dress decreases demand for fashionable clothing or the latest technology. Even more important, there is a wonderful freedom from the highly privatized view of wealth borne out of a consumerist paradigm among these companions along the road of faith. While they do not share a common purse, wealth is looked on through communal glasses. One man in their community passed away, leaving his family with some debts. The rest of this small community pooled their resources, paid off the obligations, and set up the widow and her children in a sustainable farming operation. The year prior to our arrival, a person in the larger, nationwide strain of this particular Old Order racked up a catastrophic health care bill of $750,000. Congregations around the country took up an offering and paid the entire hospital bill without needing to mortgage their churches or halt their missions. In fact, David told me that this cluster of eighteen families probably sends someone to Wales, where they are serving to plant and support a budding Old Order community, about six times per year.

We were also impressed to see the way they loved and cared for those among them who had special needs. There are four or five in this small communion of believers who have physical or developmental challenges. These community members with disabilities were as thoroughly part of the life of the body as anyone else in the fellowship. A deaf boy, for instance, was able to experience a normal school life without any special instruction or state-funded assistance because all the other boys in his school learned sign language so they could take turns translating the lessons and include him in extracurricular activities. Even the "needy" were not needy in this community. If there were a mathematical formula that calculated some combination of material wealth and relational wealth, then I would guess this community would beat, hands down, any rich suburban neighborhood in the industrialized world.

I am not saying that this community is a perfect representation of the idyllic church and its mission. The people we lived with for a short time readily admitted that they were broken and sinful and likely had many things wrong. But their commitment to each other, to simplicity and to a shared vision of the Christian faith bore witness to the power of Christian community. Most of us in the West have forgotten that we need one another. We were created in community by a God who exists in community to live in interdependence with one another and our Maker. When we forget this, when we become masters of our own destiny, we cut ourselves off from a primary aspect of our design and become adrift as individuals in a sea of individuals.

We were created in community by a God who exists in community to live in interdependence with one another and our Maker.

Putting "Y'all" Back in Scripture

Thomas Cahill, in his epic book *How the Irish Saved Civilization,* describes St. Augustine as the first, true autobiographer. Referring to Augustine's *Confessions,* Cahill says, "human consciousness takes a quantum leap forward—and becomes self-consciousness. Here for the first time is a man consistently observing himself not as Man but as this singular man—Augustine."[2]

There is within the gospel a deep appreciation for the individual. Each person is fearfully and wonderfully made, and each person must give an account. Our individual deeds and our faith as a singular person have consequences. This is not lost on the Protestant evangelical. What is lost on many evangelicals, especially those of us from the West, is not that God speaks to and interacts with us as individuals but that God exists in the plural throughout the Scriptures and interacts most frequently with communities.

From the very first page of Scripture we begin to get a taste for the communal nature of God and those made in God's image. "Then God said, 'Let us make humankind in our image, according to our likeness'" (Genesis 1:26). While God may be one, as the majority of human beings on earth today would profess,[3] God is not singular, at least not according to Genesis 1. The Christian faith asserts that God exists in three persons— Father, Son and Holy Spirit, and that both the male and the female reflect the image of God equally. God exists in community, created in community, rules in community and is present within community. The only thing in God's good creation that was not good was the aloneness of the first human, "It is not good that the man should be alone" (Genesis 2:18). The cruelest torture designed by humanity is solitary confinement. Without regular interaction with others, we go insane. There is a profound communal orientation for the Godhead as well as for those made in God's image. We do not seem to be able to exist (at least not for long) outside of a social structure.

The English language, coupled by a growing emphasis on individualism, has robbed much of the communal orientation of Scripture. There are forty-seven hundred verses in the Bible where the plural *you* has been translated simply as "you" in English,[4] and this can feed our individualism.

For surely I know the plans I have for y'all, says Yahweh, plans for y'all's welfare and not for harm, to give y'all a future with hope. (Jeremiah 29:11, with Texas Bible extension)

The Texas translation of Jeremiah 29:11 has attempted to redress the universal use of *you* in places where the original language is plural by using *y'all* wherever the Greek or Hebrew is addressing a community. Many of us from a modernist, individualist society have completely obliterated the original meaning of thousands of verses like Jeremiah 29:11. We have taken God's Word addressed to a group and particularized those verses to us as individuals. Or perhaps it is more accurate to say we have appropriated verses intended for a community not only to an individual but to a particular individual, namely, *me*. In this example we like to confer on ourselves personally God's corporate plan to prosper exiled Israel. While there may indeed be a sense in which God has a vision or plan for individuals, this is not what the verse here is stating. God is speaking about a communal vision for wellness and shalom. This promise is not conferred on any one particular individual, nor is it intended for each individual within the community; the promise is for the nation as a collective, and it is this collective understanding of God's peace with human communities and their peace with one another that rings throughout the Scriptures. Israel is not so much a grouping of individuals but "a people," and there's a difference. A group of individuals does not necessarily share an identity or a destiny. God's people are most often dealt with in the united plural. The corporate body of Israel was judged, exiled, forgiven and redeemed as a whole. God dealt with Gentile nations as a collective as well. Nineveh, in the time of Jonah, stood in danger of judgment for its communal sins. Judgment was averted when the community repented as a collective and turned from "the violence that is in their hands" (Jonah 3:8). We have so boiled down communal good or communal sin into the individual good and the individual sin that it is difficult for us to even conceptualize God relating to entire cities or nations as if they were one.[5]

The New Testament captures a sense of collectivism in the metaphor of a single body made up of many parts (Romans 12; 1 Corinthians 10; 12) and in living stones being built into one spiritual house (1 Peter 2:5) or in the church as one bride being wed to Jesus Christ (Revelation 19; 21–22). What's more, Jesus pronounces woes on entire cities, some of which were really nation-states, for their collective sins. Peter refers to the New Testament faith community in the same collective voice that God speaks of Israel in the Old Testament: the billions who make up the church today are a "holy nation, God's own people [singular]" (1 Peter 2:9). On the whole, Scripture deals with the individual only within the context of the communal.

THE FRAYED HUMAN ROPE

Since the beginning of human history we have always regarded ourselves in the plural. Shame assigned to one member of the family was shame conferred on the entire clan. In ancient societies, your father and your tribal affiliation were part of your identity—part of your name, your personhood. Our conception of personhood has nearly always been understood within the framework of a community, whether as extended family or clan or tribe. We were wired to perceive ourselves in a communal context. But for just the thinnest sliver of the human race, in only the most recent seconds of human history, a few of us have begun to unravel from each other. Some ethnicities are managing to hold on to a modicum of communal orientation even while living in the West. Many of my American friends of African, Asian or Latin American heritage, for instance, relate to their cousins at a higher level of intimacy and contact that I relate to my siblings. But even this is diminishing as we become increasingly mobile and less interwoven with our clans. Loneliness in the West is beginning to take on epidemic proportions as the social fabric we were meant to operate in becomes frayed. A record 35 percent of Americans over the age of forty-five report being chronically lonely,[6] and 28 percent of the US population lives in one-person households, the highest percentage in recorded history.[7] A one-person household? Not that long ago, even for white folks, a "one-person household" would have been an oxymoron. For my grandparents the term *household* by necessity consisted of more than one person. This is still true today for much of the world who shares a roof with aunts, uncles, cousins, grandparents and the occasional distant relation.

For just the thinnest sliver of the human race, in only the most recent seconds of human history, a few of us have begun to unravel from each other.

I tied a twenty-foot rope swing onto a high branch of our maple tree some years back. Over time the end of the rope has begun to fray and the swing seat came off, much to the surprise of the ten-year-old neighbor boy using the swing (who, thankfully, landed squarely on his feet). I attempted to reattach the seat. It was nearly impossible to pull together the individual threads that at one time comprised a single rope and pass it through the hole in the center of the seat in order to make a new knot. Once the tightly woven filaments of the rope separate, the fraying works its way up the rope, and what was once a sturdy cable has become a mass of twisted, dangling threads shooting off in all different directions and making it hard to gain the original integrity of the rope. On their own the individual strands were practically useless to me. I needed a closely bound collective of strands in order to tie the knot that would hold the seat.

Individualism versus collectivism has always existed as a tension within and between societies; it's just that in recent centuries the political, economic and military strength has followed individualist countries. The influence of these cultures has exerted great pressure on the rest of the world. Now, living alone in a city of millions has appeared as a strange new blip on the outer edge of the anthropological radar screen. And this lonesome reality is advancing quickly toward the center. Our families, tribes and clans are unraveling.

The journey away from collectivism and toward individualism has been served by capitalism, which turns private ownership into a way of thinking about all things. In the Bible there is an expectation that the human fabric is held together by a larger understanding of communal responsibility. A clan-based structure tethered the financial and social responsibility of hundreds together. Boaz's responsibility to Naomi and her daughter-in-law Ruth was tied together by kinship, even though he did not know this family. Capitalism has accelerated our ability to exist with very little need for interdependence. Wealth, under capitalism, is no longer a national, clan-based or even a nuclear-family commodity—it can be exclusively assigned to one individual. The corporate vision is that the collective (the corporation) serves the individual (the investor), not the other way around. At least we must acknowledge that profit for the investor is the governing principle in corporate capitalism. Advancing the income and status of the individual investor is the final and ultimate trump card.

We no longer need one another in the ways we needed each other just a few centuries ago. Even married couples can possess different bank accounts and own different items while living in the same home. This individuation of money and possessions has never before occurred on the scale at which it is happening, and over the course of the past five hundred years the extreme privatization of nearly all aspects of life is becoming the norm. While it is impossible to draw a straight line between our highly individualized society and corporate-styled capitalism or the Protestant Reformation, I cannot help but notice the ways in which individualism has made itself at home in the corporate world and in the Protestant faith.

A Privatized Faith

Great Britain, the Netherlands, Switzerland and Germany—the cultural womb of Protestantism—rank among the most individualistic on the individualism-collectivism continuum. It should be no surprise then that the Protestant expression of Christianity possess such strong individualistic elements. Not only was the faith born out of a sense of empowering the individual to read and interpret the Bible for oneself, but Protestantism took root in the world's most culturally individualistic countries at that time. This culturally individualist overlay placed on the Christian faith by northern European Protestant architects has come to impose an individualist worldview on nearly everyone who has come under the Protestant ideology.

In seventeenth-century America the introduction of a second church in a town that previously had only one church for everyone proved a great dilemma. Before that time it was assumed that a resident would worship at whatever Christian church had been established in a town or village, regardless of the denomination. Neighbors and workmates would quite likely share the Communion table, no matter how they may have differed in theology. But a second church meant there was a choice. One family might attend one church and their neighbor might attend another, changing the nature of that relationship and allowing them to privatize their faith just a bit more. The human chord of home, work and church unraveled a little further. James Hudnut-Beumler, professor of American religious history at Vanderbilt University, notes that a second church in town "was traumatic because it represented a breakdown in a prior and cherished communal form of life. It introduced the market and choice to a place (religious life) where most would have thought it undesirable, even unnatural."[8]

Today, most Protestants expect they will have a variety of choices for a house of worship, and that their choice of where to go to church is primarily an individual matter. Not only might they choose a house of worship based solely on personal preferences, but they might decide to switch churches several times in the course of their life whether their physical address changes or not. Even in a household where every member shares the Christian faith, mother, father, daughter and son may attend different houses of worship.

My faith choices are nearly completely private ones, which I make to satiate my own private needs. God speaks to me alone, and I give to God my worship mainly as a private affair—even if I do so in a room with others. Salvation and baptism are among the most privatized aspects of the Protestant faith, yet they appear in the New Testament on several occasions as communal experiences (Cornelius's household [Acts 11:14]; Lydia's household [Acts 16:15]; Philippian jailer's household [Acts 16:31]; Crispus's household [Acts 18:8]; Stephanas's household [1 Corinthians 1:16]). In the first century of the church's existence, households believed and were typically baptized as a community; such was the communal mindset of ancient Near East. Protestants, however, have left very little room for groups to choose to follow Christ, not primarily because of theology, though there is a place for individual decisions and consequences (see Ezekiel 18), but because of our culturally informed individualistic bias. We are uncomfortable with the notion of communal conversion because we have allowed culture to govern theology, not the other way around. Protestants generally invite individuals to accept Jesus as their "personal" Lord and Savior, as if the relationship between the person and Jesus should not be cluttered by our communal ties.

Protestant missionaries from the West often bump into this challenge in the parts of the world that value collectivism. Western missionaries can sometimes instruct collectivistic cultures from their individualistic perspective.

E. Randolph Richards, a Southern Baptist missionary to Indonesia from 1988 to 1996, was asked to weigh in on a serious church matter. A young, faithful, Indonesian Christian couple who had relocated from their home village years earlier now wanted to join the local church. They had attended this church faithfully and lived exemplary lives, but they had left their home village because of a gross misstep: they had married for love, without the consent of their parents. Having broken such critical relationships, should they be able to join this church? Richards was a bit bewildered. Marriage is an individualistic decision, isn't it? The individualistic-collectivistic continuum was in conflict as the American missionary and the Indonesian elders both approached the same Scriptures from different worldviews. Richards had been brought up to understand that important life decisions are made individualistically, which was the lens he brought to the Scriptures. The elders, who viewed life through the lens of collectivism, wondered if Richards had ever read the apostle Paul, who counseled children to obey parents. Writing in his book *Misreading Scripture with Western Eyes* (coauthored with Brandon O'Brien), Richards admits, "I suddenly found myself wondering if I had, in fact, ever really read Paul. My 'American Paul' clearly did not expect his command to include adult children deciding whom to marry."[9]

Of course most cultural artifacts are neither right nor wrong. Time orientation is neither morally better nor more corrupt than event orientation.[10] The same can be said of individualism or collectivism. They simply are what they are, cultural preferences, and individualistic perspectives need a place at the interpretive table. But when someone convinced of the certainty of individualism imposes this cultural value uncritically on collectivist cultures, it impedes the authentic expression of the faith among those who are wired differently. Amoral cultural preferences infused with moral value can imprison the imagination and end up fanning the flames of ethnocentrism and imperialism.

> Amoral cultural preferences infused with moral value can imprison the imagination and end up fanning the flames of ethnocentrism and imperialism.

A student from Saudi Arabia who lived with our family for a couple of years regularly used our possessions without asking permission as if they were his own. And of course, they were his own—or rather, he had become part of our family collective and therefore all possessions (including his) were held in common by all. Private ownership means something very different in Middle Eastern cultures. "Private" may include a rather large circle. In Western culture private ownership has been placed on steroids. Many of us have come to overly privatize our material possessions, our faith confessions and the choice of our profession.

The Leader as Individual

The corporate worldview has shaped how we approach employment and how we view the relationship between employee and employer. Gone (for the most part) are the days of the family farm, the cottage industry, and the guilds and trade associations a person might have been born (or pressed by the family) into. The individualist culture highly affirms each person making a private decision about his or her career, and generally frowns on parents or peers influencing that process. Most of us apply for a job as an individual. We are hired under some kind of contractual arrangement whereby we provide our labor in exchange for wages. There are people I may want to consider or consult when choosing a job, but by and large I make the choice independently.

Protestant missions are no different. Individuals mostly choose to work for a church, a mission agency or a nonprofit based on a personal sense of fit with the organization. My relationship to my employer, InterVarsity Christian Fellowship, is contractual, not covenantal nor familial. It is a kind of business arrangement. Decision making within our business-patterned organizations also tend to follow a fairly individualistic approach. While there is some sense of team, individualistic organizations may allow many to express their opinion, but at the end of the day a decision is made hierarchically. If an individual does not like the decision, he or she is free to leave the organization. The brave maverick leader that goes against the tide of popular opinion in order to make a decision based on his or her individual conscience is exalted in Western culture. And this is the filter through which we see all the great leaders in Scripture, so we tend to sanctify this version of leadership to the exclusion of leaders who approach decision making more communally. It is one more way that a very northern European, corporate, business-oriented perspective has come to rule our vision.

I often find both in the church and in the nonprofit world that leadership bends toward a very specific personality, one that resembles Donald Trump and type-A leaders like him rather than people who may take a more collective approach. How do we create space for another kind of decision making or leadership while still recognizing the value of the more individualistic, type-A leader?

QUAKING THE INDIVIDUALIST DECISION-MAKING MODEL

Protestants in the seventeenth century didn't like religious protesters who didn't protest institutional religion in quite the same way as Luther, Calvin and Zwingli protested institutional religion. Like the Anabaptist movements, Quakers were a community of believers who drew out of the Scriptures a vision of the Christian faith different from Catholics and the state-sponsored Protestant movements. They were hated, harassed, hunted and hanged by the guardians of Protestant theology in much the same fashion that the great-grandparents of these Protestant inquisitors may have been by the Catholics.

Remarkably, Quakers come from some of the most culturally individualistic people on earth, the English, and yet they practice such a radically communal form of decision making. Now to be sure, Quakers have incorporated their individualistic cultural moorings into their theology. God, according to Quakers, is capable of speaking to each individual in the quiet of his or her heart without reference to others. Faith is very much a deeply personal and privatized experience. But at the same time the Quakers practice a thoroughgoing form of communalism to make decisions. When Quakerism came onto the scene in the mid-1600s, there was a "subordination of all individual leadings to the control of the community, a belief that the Spirit's voice in the gathered community was more reliable than the Spirit's voice within oneself."[11]

A Quaker business meeting is anything but businesslike, at least in the ways twenty-first-century corporations conduct business meetings. Quaker meetings have no leader, and the start and finish of each meeting is conducted in absolute silence. A clerk may preside, bring up various items of business either submitted beforehand or brought up in the meeting, but otherwise everybody's word stands on equal footing. Arguing in support of a particular solution to a problem is frowned upon.

"The mere gaining of debating points is found to be unhelpful and alien to the spirit of worship which should govern the rightly ordered Meeting." How can the common good be discerned if "great rhetoric or clever argument" pushes people's opinions this way and that?[12] Rather, people should seek to listen more than speak, and when they do speak they should use simple and unadorned language so as not to manipulate others based on emotion or cajoling. Absolute unanimity may not be possible, but it is possible to discuss a matter until the general sense of the community is discerned. "When a course of action receives the general, though not necessarily unanimous, approval of the group, the presiding clerk formulates the sense of the meeting and it is recorded in the minutes. No vote is taken; there is no decision made by a majority, who override opposition. Action is taken only when the group can proceed in substantial unity."[13]

Meetings with no persuading, no leaders and no voting: from our modern corporate sensibilities this is no way to run an organization. But then again, Quakers didn't want a corporate-shaped organization; they wanted to follow Christ, without placing a chain of command between the congregation and the voice of God. They were to act, as best they could, as a collective, listening together to God without senior pastor, chief executive or board of directors having final say. It may seem to us to be a very inefficient way to move something forward, but in fact the Quakers were very effective Protestant missionaries long before people like William Carey, the Judsons or even George and Hannah Leile.

The story of the early Quakers is a sad and checkered tale of a community of men and women sending communities of missionaries around the world urging people to submit themselves to the still, small voice of God's Spirit rather than to human kings. While their individualistic strain of heeding only the "Inner Light" may have led some away from orthodox

> **Meetings with no persuading, no leaders and no voting: from our modern corporate sensibilities this is no way to run an organization.**

convictions about the historicity of Christ's death and resurrection, they
have provided us with a picture of culturally individualistic Christians em-
bracing communal forms of organization and decision making that bear
heeding. What might the mission of the church look like if we, like the
church in Antioch (Acts 13), took the time to fast, pray and listen to the
Spirit together? Might the Spirit say to whole communities, "Set apart
these, and then rally to support and send them to other places"?

Western Protestant views of gifting and calling are individualized at an
exaggerated level. The emphasis is on our special and individual part in the
body, rather than on the body as a whole, in which we play a part. Richards
and O'Brien point out in *Misreading Scripture with Western Eyes* that
1 Corinthians 6:19 is usually translated and experienced from an individualistic perspective: "Do you not know that your bodies are temples of the
Holy Spirit, who is in you, whom you have received from God?" (NIV).
However, in the Greek, the *you* is plural and *temple* is singular. "Collectively, you all make up a single temple" might be how the early listeners
heard that verse. Peter uses this idea when addressing the fact that we are
collectively being built into a spiritual house (1 Peter 2:5). "We are happy
to be part of the collective as long as we are still individually recognizable.
But what went without being said for Peter and his audience—and much
of the rest of the world today—is that the emphasis is on the whole."[14]

Can we recover a biblical sense of community in a culture of individuals
making individualistic decisions to join organizations who also embrace
noncommunal forms of decision making?

LOCAL COMMUNITY AS MISSION STRUCTURE

Protestant missionaries are rarely sent out as a community from a community. Jesus paired the disciples he had been living and traveling with and
sent them out in fellowship pairs. The Antioch church sent Paul and
Barnabas, a duo who worked together over many years to build the very
church that sent them. The church community together discerned that
these two leaders were called and equipped, and the community sent and

supported the missionary team. Within the Western Protestant context, we usually decide independently that we are missionaries and apply as individuals to work with a mission organization in much the same way that we might apply to take a position with Proctor & Gamble or Walmart. We sign a contract, undertake an individualized job description, work alongside people we have never before met, and work under a supervisor we may see for the first time on the field. This is the corporate paradigm, as distinct from the more communal process of joining a guild of tradesmen or a small business. For most Protestants, we raise individual support, asking individual donors to give to our individual ministry needs. We are employed by corporate-styled organizations with a revolving door of executives and a board of directors with whom we have little to no relationship. Our lives have become more and more disconnected from others, and we have forgotten the communal approach to mission.

Mission today rarely arises out of community. Nor are we sent communally alongside those with whom we share history.

Three families from the same small, urban church in Cincinnati, Ohio, are living and working communally in a Southeast Asian context hostile to Christian mission. The story of their formation and launch into mission is a prophetic challenge to the individualized notion of mission that has dominated the Protestant church for the last two hundred years.

University Christian Church (UCC) had a penchant for developing community. Dr. Troy Jackson, who pastored UCC for nearly twenty years, encouraged the UCC community to organize themselves in order to address holistic kingdom needs. UCC created the Roh Street Café, which has become a community gathering place and a space that encourages the arts. When a church member working in a poor Guatemalan village told Les Stoneham, manager of Roh Street Café, that locals were getting just a fraction of what they should from farming coffee, Les traveled to Santa Maria de Jesus. Julio, a local coffee farmer with a vision for his community, worked with Les to spawn a cooperative among the farmers that would empower them to control their own processing and export directly to US buyers without the need for layers of middlemen. Through years of persistent effort, a cooperative emerged, farmers are now receiving a living wage, and the export brand, La Armonia Hermosa, has become well established.

One couple in the church, inspired by this vision, wondered if they could wed economic development with pioneer mission work. They began dreaming with Pastor Troy about birthing a business that would generate living wages for local workers in an area of the world where no churches and few Christians existed. They called on Frontiers to help them dream.

Frontiers, like few American mission agencies, recognizes the need to rattle the cages of existing paradigms. Despite being a parachurch mission agency that has an identity and structure distinct from a church or denomination, they have empowered dozens of churches to recruit, train and send their own communities from within the congregation. The training model they use (TOAG—Training Ordinary Apprentices to Go) involves drawing together a team from the church and then plunging them into a ten-month communal-training program locally. The team members ideally relocate to live within walking distance of one another, build healthy interdependence, and study things like the language of the place they hope to go, church planting methods, and peacemaking, all while working their day jobs. Eventually the team, along with a Frontiers leader, goes on a survey trip to their target location to scout out possible living locations and service opportunities. In the process the church is able to discern together who is called and how others in the body could support the work.

At this writing, three families, including seven children under ten (with another child on the way), are living and serving together in this foreign location. They are a community that built a history together in a US church, having been sent by the people they attended church with. It is a picture of mission from a communal orientation—people learning to love, fight and serve locally for years before being launched from their home fellowship into mission.

Freeing the Community from Individualism

Wikipedia states that "corporate personhood is the legal concept that a corporation may be recognized as an individual in the eyes of the law."[15] I find it interesting that the word *corporate* implies a community, and yet the entity itself is regarded as an individual in the eyes of the law. In the best light this may mean that a group of people under a corporation are able to achieve a sense of common identity, destiny and purpose. But how do we shed the individualistic mindset that so often works against a communal vision?

Plurality and diversity in leadership. Frank Viola argues persuasively in *Pagan Christianity?* and other places that New Testament Christianity embraced a plurality of leaders without hierarchy.[16] The assignment of an individual head pastor who leads a church community and a singular bishop with line authority over head pastors was a second-century deviation. Christ's intention for plurality in leadership was expressed in the calling of twelve apostles who were not hierarchically arranged.[17] Israel's earliest governing structure consisted of judges and elders and warnings against a singular king (1 Samuel 8). My church has existed for years without the singular leadership of a head pastor. It has operated nicely with a rotating group of elders. The mission organization Servants has crafted a structure of four chief leaders without a first among equals. Most of these leaders live on the mission field and meet virtually on a regular basis to deal with the day-to-day needs of the larger fellowship. The mission has learned to operate under a communal style, as has my church, without the need for a person to serve as tie-breaker or final authority. I believe that much more room can be made in our churches and ministries for a plurality of leaders, which eschews the need for ministry monarchs.

Many of us have also elevated a particular personality as the ideal leader. We might call this person the "type-A" leader. This narrowly defined vision of leadership often involves an aggressive, no-nonsense decision-making style that values direct confrontation. This ideal fits many culturally white, male leaders well but does not work for many others. As we work to flatten our corporate structures that bend toward the chief executive, president or head pastor, we also need to diversify our vision of leadership in order to give greater authority to skilled men and women who do not fit the dominant paradigm.

A larger place for consensus. A mission team or a church small group might encourage members to bring difficult decisions to the community under two headings. One would be a request for advice, from which the person would seriously consider the wisdom of the community but make the decision on their own. Another valid category could be an invitation for the group to come to consensus before a decision is made. We tend to shy away from this because of our love for independence and fear of a stalemate. I serve as elder for the mission Servants mentioned above. Each field team governs itself in the local situation. But important decisions for the larger organization are made roughly every eighteen months when they gather as a community from around the world. An issue is discussed and debated until there is well-nuanced and broadly embraced common understanding. They do not move forward on a decision if there is significant dissent. Those with minority opinions may choose to submit to the larger will. They have managed the dance of communal decision making without dragging issues out ad nauseam or killing the individual voice. It is possible to move forward as a community without submitting to an individualistic hierarchy.

On the importance of communal diversity. John Hayes, founder and key leader in the mission InnerCHANGE, says that it takes a community to reach a community. But John likes to emphasize the need for diversity in the communities we form. "Community should be deftly assembled in a host locale such that the community they create is first and foremost about building community with their neighbors."[18] Though the Frontiers example with University Christian Church mentioned earlier includes ethnic, gender and occupational diversity, it is not clear whether residents from the host country have been woven into the team. It is relatively easy to build community with those who are like us. It is another thing altogether to build community with people who have significantly different backgrounds, ethnicities and nationalities. In Christian mission, I have found the most robust communities are extremely diverse. Unhealthy forms of idealism are sacrificed on the altar of compromise and practicality in a diverse group. As we move away from individualism and toward a communal understanding of life and Christian mission, diversity will force us to balance the need for individual expression, culture and personality within a functional collective.

TIME FOR BIFOCALS

It was hard for me to get bifocal lenses. It is a sign of aging and the inflexibility of my eyes to perceive with clarity things near and far. But it has been a necessary adjustment in order for me to get along in life. I need to read the road sign one hundred yards away as well as the speedometer right in front of my face.

In this chapter I am not suggesting that the Protestant church should abandon a sense of individual personhood or of cultivating the intimate and personal qualities of our relationship to God. I am only calling for a change in our prescription. We have aged enough now to have lost some of our clarity when looking at the larger picture. The vision of God calling, equipping and relating to us as a communal entity has grown fuzzy. While most of the world has continued to cultivate a healthy sense of collectivism, the West has eroded the communal identity or connectedness we enjoyed a few centuries ago. We can no longer see the communal orientation in Scripture or the communal aspects of the church necessary to live and serve well with the larger Christian community. We are driving down the highway with reading glasses on, and if we fail to get lenses that allow us to see clearly at a distance as well as up close, we are going to crash our missionary vehicles.

It may also be a good time to consider sharing leadership in a more integral way with the African, Asian and Latin American leaders who continue to live on the world's margins. After all, those on the margins of the systems and structures of this world are often in the center of God's kingdom.

6

FROM MAINSTREAM TO MARGIN

The high school my kids attended is a little on the edge of the norm in Wisconsin. In a state that is over 80 percent white and a city that is more than three-quarters white, Madison East High is mostly nonwhite. It is the most diverse of the city's public high schools, both economically and ethnically. But what's really interesting to me about Madison East is that the popularity pecking order appears to be reversed from most other high schools, certainly the one I attended. The somewhat brainy, nerdy students make up the drama crowd, and the kids in Show Choir, East High's version of a glee club, are among the most popular and envied students in the school. By contrast, the football players and cheerleaders don't occupy very prominent spots on the social ladder.

When our eldest daughter, Hannah, graduated high school, her class unanimously chose the school janitor to deliver the keynote address at the commencement ceremony. Mr. Ely was well-loved by students and teachers alike, and this was his final school year as janitor. He was stepping into retirement after thirty years of humble service in the hallways of the school. His message that day to the students of East was as countercultural as the student body's choice of speaker. While many other high school commencement speakers would be charging graduates to step out, move up and change the world, Mr. Ely readily admitted that he had spent his entire life living in just one zip code. His challenge to the students: settle down, plant roots, love their neighbors and give themselves to one, small, obscure patch of the planet.

I found the address of this person, whom most of America would assign to society's margins, powerful and moving. The call to "lead a quiet and peaceable life in all godliness and dignity" (1 Timothy 2:2) is hard to hear above the din of voices beckoning us to seize the day, rock the world and make something of ourselves. But it is often from the edges of society that great things emerge.

There is a curious, ancient thread running through the mythologies of nearly every ethnic grouping on earth. It sometimes involves the high king or chief or emperor disguising himself and living among commoners. Or it is the legend of a peasant girl who becomes princess. Sometimes this primeval story takes the form of a popular and powerful figure who turns out to be a poseur and a person of no import. In either case, those on the margins of society in these tales are revealed actually to be at the center, or someone at the center is exposed as insignificant.

Why is it that so many people over such a broad geography and time span share such a deeply ingrained suspicion that things which appear to be preeminent are actually insignificant, and that which seems unimportant is actually central? The human psyche is programmed to be suspicious of the nature of reality and the world's definitions of what's at the core and what's at the periphery.

The Scriptures fuel this suspicion. The choosing of Israel's archetypal king, David, is one example. The prophet Samuel was called by God to anoint one of the sons of Jesse as king. After seeing the physique of David's oldest brother Eliab, Samuel concludes this must be the king. But God told him, "Do not

> **The human psyche is programmed to be suspicious of the nature of reality and the world's definitions of what's at the core and what's at the periphery.**

look on his appearance or on the height of his stature, because I have rejected him; for the LORD does not see as mortals see; they look on the outward appearance, but the LORD looks on the heart" (1 Samuel 16:7).

Instead, Israel's greatest king was plucked from the pasture, where he had been relegated to one of the most marginalized professions of his day: tending sheep.

In the story of Esther, not only is an obscure yet beautiful girl born of a hated ethnic group chosen for queen, but the popular right-hand man to the king, Haman, is rejected in favor of the socially invisible and lowly Mordecai, Esther's uncle.

Throughout the Bible we are regularly confronted with the notion that the "center" for most turns out to be on God's margin, and those considered marginal by everyone else turn out to be at God's center. Perhaps the ultimate account of core-periphery confusion is the story of Jesus of Nazareth. Of all the possible avenues for God's good invasion of earth, of all the potential incarnational story lines with any sort of rationality, the nativity of Jesus Christ is the least sensible, at least by the world's standards. I could possibly envision God appearing in the first century as the humble son of a Roman emperor whose kindness and wisdom woo the empire, or God being born into the home of Herod, turning that corrupt lineage around. I could even appreciate the incarnation of Messiah into one of the great high priestly families using his wealth and privilege to bless the nations. But that God was born in the household of a peasant couple whose reputation had been marred by the unplanned pregnancy of an unwed teenage girl is fringe indeed. That this God baby was laid in the feeding trough of an animal due to the family's poverty and raised as a working-class stiff in a backwater town among an occupied and defeated people? This is no way to convey one's cosmic supremacy to the world. Jesus' marginality is a sign to us. It is an invitation for those of us in the center to look for our salvation from the unexpected, hidden and even despised places.

Privilege and disadvantage are reversed in the Christ story. Those who are privileged in God's economy are the dirty shepherds sleeping outdoors like animals. They were the first humans to whom the favor of God and the birth of Messiah were announced. Esteemed in the Christ story are the tax collectors and sex workers. Those who would never be admitted into a religious community actually traveled together with this wandering rabbi, as his students. Venerated in the Gospels are the disabled and the socially shunned, those who are never picked first for the sports team, who never get asked to prom, who are relegated to a life of beggary. The fact that the cornerstone event of the Christian faith, Christ's resurrection, was first witnessed by women, whose testimony would not be valid in a court of law in that day, is an indication of how our perceptions of margin and center are not shared by God. Poor, blind, lame and leper: these are the advantaged "class" in the kingdom of God. Wise, noble, wealthy, powerful: these have a handicap in the real world of Christ's domain. Jesus' words often shocked and offended common notions of who was blessed and who was accursed. "Truly I tell you, it will be hard for a rich person to enter the kingdom of heaven" (Matthew 19:23).

The mission of God remained on the margins of empire for the first three centuries of the church. It has always operated best on society's fringe, and some of its most successful advocates have been the socially or geographically marginalized. Whether first-century slaves, Welsh coal miners or modern-day Dalits, the most successful orientation of God's mission has always arisen from and flowed toward the world's disenfranchised.[1]

> **Poor, blind, lame and leper: these are the advantaged "class" in the kingdom of God.**

CHRIST OUTSIDE THE GATE

As Protestants we have worked hard to locate ourselves in society's center. We often rejoice when we gain the visibility of political office and thrill to a celebrity's profession of faith. In general we do not invite onto center stage the janitor, the homeless or the sex worker. We relish creating our own centers—behavioral, cultural and religious—to which we demand that those interested in the faith must come.

In *Christ Outside the Gate: Mission Beyond Christendom*, Orlando

Costas argues that in Israel's eschatological orientation the priests invited those on the periphery (the Gentile nations) to come into the center (Mount Zion), so that the outsiders might learn the ways of the God who saves.[2] Generally, they were not orientated to going themselves to the margins. The Jewish–Industrial Complex they created was safe from the defilement of the profane. Even in exile, even when ordered by God to put down roots in sacrilegious Babylon (Jeremiah 29), the Israelites still looked to Zion as the center that the ungodly nations must go to. They never quite understood the passionate heart of their Creator for the "other," the nations existing outside of the holy center they had crafted, nations to which God had desired them to go.

The strategy was to create an alternative holy world within this profane world, a world cocooned from the evils of the heathen. One that operates in righteousness and justice. This is a strategy employed in many Protestant churches' and Christian communities' attempts to live out a prophetic alternative, into which they invite others. But in the process we simply wall off ourselves from a world we are meant to fill and to satisfy. We have failed to learn the secret of being in the world without becoming of the world, and so we simply create our own little semi-Christianized version of the world. Those who are marginal to our churches and missions may be targets for our philanthropy, but they rarely become key architects of church and mission.

In chapter five I praised one of those Protestant communities that has created a prophetic alternative world: the Old Order Mennonites. There is much in their life together I would like to emulate. However, the Old Order communities hold an insular vision of church, one I struggle to fully embrace. These communities are so utterly "other," often rural and relatively unengaged in any significant way with the communities surrounding them, that they provide few onramps into their vision for social transformation. They are, in essence, a snow-globe society, which can only be observed as an ornament depicting a different and impenetrable world. This notion of inviting the outside world into a protected Beloved Community, a community living out as best they can an expression of God's kingdom, is attractive. But history is rife with high-walled Christian enclaves that are co-opted and redesigned by the powers of the world.[3] Or communities that completely fail to engage and impact a broken world. How does the church live in the corporate, consumerist world without becoming of the corporate, consumerist world? How might we deconstruct the Christian-Industrial Complex, which was built using the blueprints of the Corporate-Industrial Complex? Looking to the margins may be part of the answer.

Costas suggests that the crucifixion of Christ "outside the camp," in that place of desecration far from the temple, reorients the mission of God. The holy of holies has shifted to the margins.

> The death of Jesus not only changed the location of salvation, but also clarified the nature of mission. By shifting salvation to the periphery, the mission of the people of God has undergone a complete about-face. Mission is no longer "coming" but "going" (as anticipated by Isaiah in 19:23-25). Bearing witness to God's saving grace means going to the crucified Son of God, outside the gate of our sacred compounds, to share in his suffering death for the world. This is what the author of Hebrews has in mind when he states: "Therefore let us go forth to him outside the camp, and bear the abuse he endured" (13:13). The fact that Jesus wrought salvation outside the Holy City does not mean that we have now a new fixed salvific center but, rather, a permanent, *moving* center in the periphery of life. Salvation is to be focused on that person who has assumed the perpetual identity of the outsider. We can know Jesus only as the crucified Son of God suffering and dying for the world amid the outcasts and rejects.[4]

In following after the commercial business construct for mission, Protestants are oriented around a worldview that works best for society's elite and is practically unworkable for those eking out a living on the edges of empire. If we insist on constructing church and mission around mindsets and systems most accessible to the middle and upper classes, how do we hope to find Christ who was crucified between criminals and sojourns alongside the marginalized? If church and mission structures have not completely broken free of colonial mindsets, if they require large infusions of capital, if they are principally founded on the idea of gospel as product, and if they are built on a mainly European individualistic vision of the world, then how will the burgeoning, poor, outcast, majority of this world living in barrios, favelas and bustees see that the kingdom of God is good news to them?

> **If we insist on constructing church and mission around mindsets and systems most accessible to the middle and upper classes, how do we hope to find Christ who was crucified between criminals and sojourns alongside the marginalized?**

EMPOWERING THE MARGINS OF THE EARLY CHURCH

The first leaders of the church were Jewish men. They were faithful to the Jewish law and likely had lived their whole lives among fellow Jews who likewise were pure concerning the law. While these men may not have been among the elite, they were culturally, religiously and linguistically quite close to the center of the Judean mainstream. These men, the Twelve, were in charge of the common purse, and there was enough for everyone to live well. "There was not a needy person among them, for as many as owned lands or houses sold them and brought the proceeds of what was sold. They laid it at the apostles' feet, and it was distributed to each as any had need" (Acts 4:34-35). But as the church stretched its arms around the Greek-speaking Jews from the edges of empire, a problem arose. Although the Jewish believers who had grown up in barbarian towns abroad contributed to the common fund, the money was not making its way to the poor Greek speakers who had needs. Somehow, there were no needy among them in Acts 4, but by Acts 6, with the inclusion of fringe Jews into their community, there were needy widows who were being overlooked. "But as the believers rapidly multiplied, there were rumblings of discontent. The Greek-speaking believers complained about the Hebrew-speaking believers, saying that their widows were being discriminated against in the daily distribution of food" (Acts 6:1 NLT)

Adding a marginalized community to the ranks of the church exposed the tendency for exclusionary systems to crop up even among the followers of Christ. Perhaps it was the linguistic barrier, maybe it was that the relational lines between the apostles and the Hebrew-speaking poor were better established, allowing resources to flow more freely. Whatever the case, there is no indication in the text that this exclusion and discrimination was just the perception of the excluded. It was a genuine case of the "center" taking care of their own, while leaving the margins out of the equation.

> So the Twelve called a meeting of all the believers. They said, "We apostles should spend our time teaching the word of God, not running a food program. And so, brothers, select seven men who are well respected and are full of the Spirit and wisdom. We will give them this responsibility. Then we apostles can spend our time in prayer and teaching the word." (Acts 6:2-4 NLT)

It is not that the "daily distribution of food" (Acts 6:1) was beneath the apostles, for the word used for "distribution" here, *diakonia* (deacon), is the same word used when speaking of "teaching" (or distribution) of the word (Acts 6:4). The ministry of the word and the ministry of food were both acts of service. In fact the men chosen to take over this task of handling the common purse are seen in the next chapters of Acts doing precisely what we see the apostles doing—traveling, preaching, teaching and baptizing. The Twelve, who had walked with Jesus from the start, needed to be devoted to teaching Jesus' message, as they had it directly from the Master. But to handle the problem of discrimination that had been created, they needed to release church leadership to those on the margins who were "known to be full of the Spirit and wisdom" (Acts 6:3). The Twelve at the center gave power and authority to the Seven from the fringe. All those to whom the apostles turned over the management of money have Greek names.

One of them was even born an uncircumcised Gentile but had converted to Judaism.

The apostles did not set up a coalition government where both Hebrew speakers and Greek speakers had their representatives to insure each of their widows had a voice at the table. From the list of Greek names given in verse 5, it looks very much like the responsibility to care for the whole community—Hebrew-speaking mainstream and Greek-speaking fringe—was completely surrendered to the excluded. The center empowered the margin, trusting that outsider Greek-speaking believers would not do to Hebrew-speaking widows what had been done to their widows. This proved a turning point in the Christian movement. "The word of God continued to spread; the number of the disciples increased greatly in Jerusalem, and a great many of the priests became obedient to the faith" (Acts 6:7). It would seem that one step in reversing our industrial complexes and experiencing breakthrough in our churches and missions is to invite the excluded into power, real power.

MISSIONARIES FROM THE MARGINS TO THE MARGINS

In 1822 Betsey Stockton became the first single American woman to serve as a missionary. The thing that makes this twenty-four-year-old remarkable is not the social norms she had to shatter in order to embark on an overseas journey as an unmarried missionary some sixty-five years before the famed single missionary Amy Carmichael. Nor is it her insistence that missionaries should educate the children of commoners, though this too was unusual among the Hawaiians she served. The remarkable thing about Betsey Stockton is that she was born into slavery. She served as slave to the wife of Ashbel Green, the man who became president of Princeton University. Once she had been manumitted, the only way in which she could fulfill her calling as a missionary was to accompany a missionary party as part-time domestic help. The American Board of Commissioners for Foreign Mission, which had sent the Judsons ten years earlier, didn't quite know how to categorize a black freed-slave missionary. She came to Hawaii on a contract that stated "she is to be regarded and treated neither as an equal nor as a servant," whatever that means.[5]

After a five-month journey from Princeton, New Jersey, around Cape Horn, Betsey and the missionary party finally weighed anchor just off the southeastern shore of Oahu. Massive Hawaiian men in canoes came aboard to greet the missionaries. These missionaries, with their Princeton decorum, melted with fear at the sight of these large, near naked brown men. Betsey writes in her journal, "The ladies retired to the cabin, and burst into tears; some of the gentlemen turned pale."[6] But Betsey knew that these were men with souls,

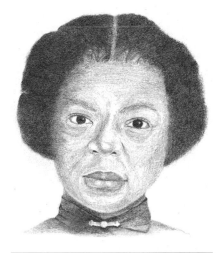

Betsey Stockton, the first single American woman to serve as a missionary. Pencil drawing by Janine Bessenecker.

made in the image of God, just like her. In a stroke of daring brilliance she scooped up the two-week old baby boy who had been born to one of the missionary couples during the journey, brought him on deck and presented him to the Hawaiian men. I am not certain how excited the parents were at what may have seemed to them like a peace offering, but the giddy delight of the Hawaiian men over the baby broke down the prejudices of the missionaries and ushered in the courage and rapport needed for them to actually disembark and begin their mission. Betsey went on to start a school among the lower-class Hawaiians. Until then only the expatriate children and the children of chieftain families were educated. For a new outbreak of kingdom to emerge it sometimes takes someone from the margins to bring a marginalized Savior to the excluded.

Up until Acts 11 the gospel had moved forward only among Jews, despite Peter's powerful conversion experience in the home of a Gentile military man named Cornelius. But in chapter 11 we meet newly empowered marginalized Jews from Cyprus and Cyrene who have the gumption to envision dirty, pork-eating barbarians entering the church. These outliers were a bit like Betsey Stockton: believers who did not naturally fit in proper, Hebrew-speaking society.

> Now those who were scattered because of the persecution that took place over Stephen traveled as far as Phoenicia, Cyprus, and Antioch, and they spoke the word to no one except Jews. But among them were some men of Cyprus and Cyrene who, on coming to Antioch, spoke to the Hellenists [other ancient authorities read *Greeks*] also, proclaiming the Lord Jesus. (Acts 11:19-20)

Cyprus and Cyrene had experienced violent ethnic tension between the Jews who were raised there and their Greek neighbors in the early decades of the first century. Believers from these parts would have known something of the challenge and exclusion of living a Jewish faith in a Gentile world. Such exclusion would have been experienced at the hands of their Hebrew-speaking brothers and sisters as well as their Gentile neighbors. Perhaps it is similar to those of minority heritage who feel "other" in a predominantly white culture and then go to their parents' or grandparents' homeland and feel "other" in that place as well because they are unfamiliar with the language and culture of their own heritage. But being a marginalized person gives one eyes to see possibilities no one else sees. Like Betsey's ability to see what majority-culture missionaries had missed, these minority culture Jews dared to imagine a church made of Gentiles.

Acts 11:26 tells us that in Antioch the disciples were first called Christians. I would suggest that before Antioch, Christians were called "Jews." In Antioch, Christianity sheds its Jewish wineskin and becomes something unrecognizable as Judaism. Here the church defies the normal trajectory of every faith rooted in one nationality or ethnicity. Egyptians had their pantheon, Greeks and Romans had their gods and goddesses, Persia and China and African tribes all had their own national deities. I am unaware of any faith before this time that was not thoroughly entrenched in an ethnic group. But when these boundary-crossing minority Jews from Cyprus and Cyrene started baptizing men and women from non-Jewish ethnicities into the faith, the followers of Messiah could no longer be called Jews—or a sect of Judaism. Only then could an identity be disentangled from the Semitic ethnicity. The ethnically Hebraic wall to the Christian faith had been breached. Christianity has remained the most nationally, ethnically and linguistically diverse faith in the world. And it started in Antioch. Jerusalem was not the birthplace of Christianity. Antioch was.

> Now in the church at Antioch there were prophets and teachers: Barnabas, Simeon who was called Niger, Lucius of Cyrene, Manaen a member of the court of Herod the ruler, and Saul. While they were worshiping the Lord and fasting, the Holy Spirit said, "Set apart for me Barnabas and Saul for the work to which I have called them." Then after fasting and praying they laid their hands on them and sent them off. (Acts 13:1-3)

This is an interesting list of leaders. Barnabas was from the island of Cyprus. He was one of the Greek-speaking Jews sent by the Jerusalem church in Acts 11 to check out the legitimacy of the sketchy Gentile church in Antioch. He may have even known some of these

Jerusalem was not the birthplace of Christianity. Antioch was.

renegade Jews who dared preach Jesus to non-Jews. Simeon, called Niger or "the black one," was likely of sub-Saharan African descent; Lucius was from Cyrene, present-day Libya, in North Africa. Manaen was from an aristocratic family and was foster-brother to Herod, the Herod John the Baptist railed against. Then there was Saul (soon to become known as Paul). He also grew up among the heathen in a town called Tarsus, which is in modern-day Turkey. Ethnically and socially most of these leaders, with the possible exception of Saul and Barnabas, were on the first-century margins of proper Jewish society—people who did not fit neatly into the confines of the Jewish-Christian sect made of Hebrew-speaking Jews living almost exclusively in a majority Jewish environment.

What follows in the remaining chapters of Acts is a record of the church becoming untethered from Jewishness, and the radical inclusion of uncircumcised, pork-eating barbarians into the family of Abraham. It was a messy work. We find Barnabas and Paul, for instance, being referred to as Zeus and Hermes by listeners who were ready to offer sacrifices to them. A moment later they left behind a church of former adherents to the Greek pantheon. It was not that Barnabas and Paul had rejected or left behind their Jewish moorings. The family of God will always trace its story through a particular people. In fact Paul and Barnabas began this journey just as Jesus began his ministry, in small-town Jewish synagogues. But from this foot in the synagogue door Paul and Barnabas often moved into the pagan corners of the empire. It was a transition from the Jewish center to the Gentile margins.

Giving power to the margins and then experiencing revival at the margins brings tension. Both the Roman Empire and the Jewish religious empire opposed the emergence of a Gentile church. It was the exclusivity of Christ over state that offended the Roman Empire, and the inclusivity of Christ to save any prostitute, tax collector or criminal that offended the Jewish empire. The calcified structures of human empire cry out in pain as they are resisted by the pressures from the excluded. To experience real breakthrough in our churches and missions we need to allow those at the edges to help us deconstruct the industrial complex.

Let us rethink our orientation to the cultural, political and social centers we have constructed for the faith, and draw into mission those who are on the margins. Otherwise we will naturally build insular systems that work well for those at the center but will exclude those on the margins.

> **The calcified structures of human empire cry out in pain as they are resisted by the pressures from the excluded.**

Outliers who could, together with those in the mainstream, break new ground and witness fresh advance. Who are the outliers in our churches and organizations, the men and women who do not fit the dominant cultural model? The Betsey Stocktons and the believers from Cyprus and Cyrene who are willing to do things others have not dared to do because they may offend majority culture sensibilities? Their position outside the dominant culture uniquely qualifies them to see things others don't see and reach into places that feel profane to us. They will create wineskins that confound or upset the current structures, but that can release the gospel of the kingdom like nothing else.

FREEING THE MARGINS FROM SLAVERY TO THE CENTER

We cannot help but to create behavioral and cultural norms in our organizations and our churches. But we can be intentional about these norms and how people who do not naturally fit them get along. We need people who do not fit our norms loaning their wisdom and their unique perspectives to our ministries. Norms do not need to be tyrants dictating all behavior, nor do they need to create impenetrable cultural fortresses around our resources and systems. Organizations in the West that have adopted or inherited a culture which is most accessible to white men will have an especially difficult time making changes, since so much of our world already pushes us in that direction. The following suggestions may bring greater health to our fellowships by releasing the assets and ingenuity of the excluded.

Empowering the margins. It would be good to review the section "Turning the purse strings over to the excluded" in chapter three. Much power in Western culture is wrapped up in our financial resources. Like the Acts 6 community, we must allow those facing the greatest financial barriers to have significant say over how we use our money. In addition, there may be ways to open ourselves up to the valuable input and involvement of members on our organizational fringe or on society's edges. People who have spent many years trapped in homelessness or the prison system have been invited to teach students as well as InterVarsity staff, despite the fact that our ministry is exclusively focused on the university campus. These men and women offer a perspective that is needed given our limited frame of reference. If your population or your ministry culture leans heavily toward one ethnic group, you could build critical mass for the underrepresented voices by inviting partners from those communities who are not formally part of your organization to join discussions. You might consider weighting the input from your ethnic minority voices so that they do not get bulldozed by the majority. Mainly, those in the cultural center need to believe that valuable input, leadership and innovation lay at the margins, and that creativity and encouragement will be needed to release those voices.

Majority culture advocates. Some who move quite easily and comfortably in the business-oriented shape of evangelical Protestantism are needed for this dismantling and reconstruction. Betsey Stockton would not have gotten far if it weren't for her former master, Ashbel Green, president of Princeton University. Green not only granted Betsey her freedom but wrote a powerful letter of recommendation urging the American Board of Commissioners for Foreign Missions to accept Betsey as a single, female missionary, something they had never done. Barnabas, Paul, Peter and others advocated strongly for the inclusion of the uncircumcised, pork-eating, Greek, barbarian church as a fully-fledged member of the Christian movement (Acts 15). We need people rooted in the majority culture to walk alongside of and then advocate for those on the fringes of our communities and on the fringes of empire.

As we grow our ability to hear from the margins of our communities and the margins of the economic and political centers of the world, we will find voices of wisdom that we have missed. But listening to those who have been excluded by the systems we have created is just the first step in building healthy interdependence. The Christian-Industrial Complex will resist what it perceives to be the vulnerability of binding our leadership, our finances and our destinies together with marginalized people.

7

FROM INDEPENDENT TO INTERDEPENDENT

I was explaining to my Filipino friend attorney Raineer Chu why some American or Western ministries choose not to absorb local Christians they are working with into their organizations. "They are reluctant to plant their flag into national workers," I told him, "adopting them into Western organizations and thereby re-creating a form of colonialism." I have seen quality local leaders snapped up into Western agencies, robbing indigenous organizations of key players. One Ethiopian friend who works with an indigenous Ethiopian ministry confided to me about the challenging choice he faced when a large American child-sponsorship organization offered him much more money and prestige than he could obtain working for a poorly resourced local ministry. He courageously decided to stay with the Ethiopian ministry, which is experiencing robust health under his leadership. But the sound of thousands of Majority World leaders being sucked into Western organizations is deafening, and it is stripping poor community churches and organizations of some of their best and brightest leaders.

Some of my Western friends who are running new mission fellowships are trying to avoid the sin of simply creating a kinder, gentler form of colonialism. "Rather," I told Raineer, "they seek to catalyze organizations which are completely indigenous and run by locals." I then referenced a local Cambodian organization that was spawned and launched by a group of Westerners. "The local organization has been fraught with challenges, but my friends prefer to act as outside catalysts and then step back, allowing the local organization to take on local workers and local boards that are separate from their Western-rooted organizations. They feel great caution integrating local organizations and workers given our colonial past, and I respect that concern."

What brother Chu said next cut me like the truth. "The explanation that the Westerners do not want to repeat colonizing the locals is artificial. . . . It is just that independence and privacy is of higher value than the value of interdependence. . . . Covering it with a nice slogan of not wanting to colonize again and not addressing the weakness of independence is sad."[1]

He is right. When we empower the margins, we want to create strict barriers so that those from the margins do not mess with the finances and leadership of organizations created by the center. The dichotomy that we must either absorb locals into our structures or allow completely local structures to emerge is a false one. It is born of similar fears inherent in the racist prohibition of mixed marriages. It is also fueled by a cultural preference for independence. Americans especially love our independence. The Declaration of Independence has shaped our psyche and fed us the lie that we are better when we don't need to depend on others nor they on us. A company, family or individual must be self-sufficient to be stable. We are happy to assimilate others into our systems, but we do not want to be dependent on anything outside our control. But the fact is that no single community, country or even continent contains all the resources and ingenuity for flourishing. We need one another, and we need each other's gifts, talents and differences in order to adequately reflect the image of God and to accomplish God's purposes. Even if that means accepting others' liabilities and limitations.

Ranieer Chu says that dependence is the mindset that rules poor countries and the organizations that arise from those communities. They are wired by centuries of domination and exploitation to believe that their only contribution is slave labor. But both the patron-client mindset in poor countries and the highly independent vision of partnership in rich ones are unbiblical. We are creatures that possess an innate need for one another in order to flourish. Procreation is very difficult alone. Interdependence is the chief vision for human relationships. We are part of a massive living organism called humanity. "No man is an island," observed John Donne. Like a scene from a horror movie, the apostle Paul describes independence in the church as a dismembered human body, with the hand or the eye attempting to sever itself from the rest of the body. Independence is a grotesque malfunction of our design.

THE ENDOWMENT EFFECT

Psychologists have observed for decades that an odd attachment seems to emerge when we own an item. It appears that we inflate the value of a thing quite significantly after it becomes "ours." While I may be willing to pay $5 for a decent coffee mug, once I come to possess it, even if I received the mug for free, I soon calculate its value somewhere around $10 and generally will not trade it for a mug of equal value. The perception of value becomes bloated in the process of ownership, a phenomenon known as the endowment effect.[2] Some sort of switch gets flipped in our brains (or, I might argue, in our souls) upon possessing something, which defies the powers of reason. We are able to exercise some rational thought when calculating the value of an item—until it becomes ours. After that, the possession spikes in value beyond all reason. It is a bit like the hypnotic hold that the One Ring in the *Lord of the Rings* trilogy exerts on its owners. When something becomes mine, it becomes precious beyond reckoning.

Recently, however, Coren Apicella and Edwardo Azevedo, two young assistant professors at the University of Pennsylvania, discovered something curious. They tested the endowment effect on the Hadza, a relatively isolated hunter-gatherer tribe in Tanzania.[3] The two researchers

> Like a scene from a horror movie, the apostle Paul describes independence in the church as a dismembered human body.

expected to find that this effect was hardwired into the human psyche, and therefore would be fully operational in people who live much closer to our ancient ancestors. This was true for the Hadza who live near urban areas. But they were surprised by the fact that the Hadza who lived nomadic lives away from a capitalist economy were impervious to the endowment effect. After gaining ownership of an item, these nomadic Hadza were perfectly willing to trade it for items of equal worth without inflating its value. Private ownership did not affect their perspective regarding the value of a thing. They were resistant to being possessed by their possessions.

Consumerism celebrates attachment to our things, but if the Hadza are any reflection of our primal design, it does not appear that we are biologically programmed this way. The closest cousins to our premodern selves operate in a highly interdependent society, such that private ownership does not hold the same power over their thinking. "Things come and go in hunter gatherer life," Coren says about the Hadza. "You don't even own that much to begin with."[4] The survival of individuals depends on the collective in ways lost upon those of us living in societies that are WEIRD (Western, educated, industrialized, rich and democratic). A hunter who kills an animal and then hoards it for himself will not fare well when fellow tribesmen score kills on days when he is without and needs someone to share. Private ownership is not a practical plan in societies where interdependence is necessary for survival.

Creating churches and organizations where finances and leadership are blended from two or more entities is far too rare. It is as if we are allergic to the thought of creating interdependence between mainstream monies and leadership from those on the periphery. I think that the endowment effect works with organizations as it does with individuals. We value beyond reason the resources our organizations possess, so we would rather spawn a completely separate entity than mix our precious resources with those of other organizations. Our actions say, "Let's keep our congregations, our youth groups and our ministries clearly separate. Let our lawyers craft carefully worded memorandums of understanding so that our money and people and ideas are unmistakably owned by one entity."

Raineer Chu went on,

I cannot overstate the need for interdependence. From it all things rise and fall. When the Americans were here, we had OMF foreign and OMF Philippines. The same was true with the Conservative Baptists and the Bible Society. Others were worse. They never even bothered to create a local organization. There is a fear of mingling finances, economic practices and leadership. There are many accounts of Filipinos having to fight for their right to be equal.

The most painful part is to be told that we are equal and then to have the Americans step out to be separate yet equal. Americans can never work together with Filipinos. When you say it is fraught with problems, I fully agree. It is messy. But to take the road that is easier is abdicating the work of unity in the body where there is now no male, female, rich, poor, Jew, Gentile, Chinese, Filipino, American, black, free, slave, etc.

The challenge for Americans is to come alongside and be a partner, and work together in the mess and demonstrate to the world that Christianity works. Don't hide behind slogans.[5]

COMPETITION IN THE KINGDOM

Some of our desire to keep our churches and organizations clearly separated stems from a spirit of competition. Competition is the lifeblood of consumerism. If there is competition in the kingdom of God it is of a different nature than the competition created in the consumerist world we live in. Romans 12:10 says, "Outdo one another in showing honor." There is far greater preference for cooperation than for competition in the Scriptures. The reality that some churches actively compete for the same

people reveals the extent to which the for-profit worldview has shaped
who we have become.

The great steel tycoon Andrew Carnegie said of the law of competition,

> It is here; we cannot evade it; no substitutes for it have been found;
> and while the law may be sometimes hard for the individual, it is best
> for the race, because it insures the survival of the fittest in every de-
> partment. We accept and welcome, therefore, as conditions to which
> we must accommodate ourselves, great inequality of environment;
> the concentration of business, industrial and commercial, in the
> hands of a few; and the law of competition between these, as being
> not only beneficial, but essential to the future progress of the race.[6]

Perhaps Carnegie could not see the trajectory for the law of competition
and where it might take us. In a day of predatory pricing, hostile takeovers
and mom-and-pop businesses being crushed by big-box stores, competition can actually create environments where some corporations become
too big to fail and are nearly immune to the threat of other businesses.

But this is not (or should not) be the case for those of us who are
seeking first God's kingdom and its righteousness. Our relationship with
other churches or ministries should be defined by collaboration—or to
take Raineer Chu seriously, defined by building interdependence. If we
need business competition, then let's compete to outdo one another in
the business of love. While not generally very lucrative in this world, it is
profitable in the kingdom. Running the race of faith in order to win the
prize (1 Corinthians 9:24) is the sort of competition Paul spoke of.
"Business will always concentrate on production, competition, and the
bottom line; religious faith will be
more concerned with distribution,
community and the finish line."[7]

If we need business competition, then let's compete to outdo one another in the business of love.

How can we develop the collab-
orative spirit of interdependence in
a world of competition?

SHARING POWER WITH THE POOR IN SPIRIT

Raineer Chu calls those of us who live and work in places of wealth to come and learn from the poor. They often have a perspective on life that most closely reflects the kingdom of God. The materially poor are quite often the poor in spirit, which may be why Jesus says, "Blessed are the poor," in Luke's sermon on the plain (the Greek word here indicates material poverty), and he says, "Blessed are the poor in spirit," in Matthew's Sermon on the Mount. They are destined to inherit the kingdom. It makes sense that Christians from places of worldly power might overturn the tables of the Christian-Industrial Complex by inviting our poor sisters and brothers into positions of authority. In his book *Kissing the Leper*, Brad Jersak talks about some of the pastors ordained at Fresh Wind Christian Fellowship in Abbotsford, British Columbia.[8] A couple of their pastors are learning-disabled men who have an uncanny ability to blurt out just the right Scripture at incredibly apropos moments. The fellowship has recognized the gift of the Spirit evidenced in these believers' lives and invited them into places of pastoral authority. Like everybody who has a mixture of assets and liabilities, there is need to discern appropriate boundaries and limitations for these men, but they are full of the Spirit and possess valuable spiritual wisdom even though their intellect will not win them any advanced degrees. Why not recognize their spiritual authority with the kind of title and responsibility befitting their unique gift? Until we break out of the conventional wisdom handed down to us by a status-distorted world, we will remain trapped in the thinking that empowers those who already have worldly power and ignores those with true kingdom authority.

My friend Bob Ekblad has built an interdependent fellowship of people on the margins with people in the mainstream. They call it Tierra Nueva—New Earth—and it is a bit of a picture of the new heavens and new earth promised in Revelation 21–22. One of their key leaders, Julio, is like those mentioned in Revelation 21 bringing the "glory and honor of the nations" into their community. But Julio comes from a different corner of society than most organizational leaders.

Bob met Julio nearly twenty years ago in the Sagit County Jail, where Bob serves as chaplain. Bob described him as a "scrappy gang member from Stockton, California, caught up in PCP and crack cocaine addiction and dealing drugs for income."[9] The two forged a keen friendship, and after Julio was released from prison, Bob would visit him in the apartment where Julio continued to deal drugs. "Our Bible studies," says Bob, "were constantly interrupted by customers wanting to buy drugs—many of whom I knew from jail Bible studies. Julio invited everyone who came by to join in and learn about God." But life on the margins can be incredibly unstable. Julio eventually moved to Arizona, where he smuggled people across the border as a coyote. It was difficult to stay in touch since Julio used a series of phones and new numbers due to his work. In their sporadic calls Julio confessed that his drug addiction was destroying his health and his soul. He had become weary of the life he was living.

In 2013 Julio called Bob to come pick him up. He'd taken a bus back to Washington. "I'm ready to surrender to Jesus and to work with you at Tierra Nueva!" Julio is working toward ordination in the community and, along with other ex-offenders who help lead Tierra Nueva, provide a critical perspective for the ministry. Their voices carry authority. Their street smarts add a kind of wisdom to the staff from the mainstream, which shapes their ministry decisions. Staff from the mainstream, connected to people with power and capital, grant access for the community to resources and other kinds of knowledge that makes this "New Earth" an amazing amalgam of gifted people.

The Mosaic community in Mexico City, of which Philip and Beauty are part (see chapter 3), wrestles regularly with the challenges of integrating mainstream workers with those who've grown up on the margins. James, an American on Mosaic's leadership board, suggested that people from the West should no longer hold leadership positions in the Mosaic community. "That's a simple excuse for not wanting to get your hands dirty and suffer the pains of leadership," said Oscar, a Mexican leader on the same team. "We don't just need you here as an alongsider, we need you to exercise your gifting and the fullness of your leadership. We need you to step out in faith and work collaboratively with the rest of us. There's already so few of us with this kind of holistic vision, so we need you to be involved fully and lead without restraint."[10]

The arrogant need the broken in order to expose the shortcomings of worldly success. Likewise, those who are locked out of the systems of this world need those with access to power and resources in order to, together, transform systems and structures. Fellowship between rich and poor can help illumine the poverty of the wealthy and the richness of the poor. The truth is that we need one another, and not always in the ways we imagine. The poor don't primarily need the wealth of the rich—though some redistribution can be helpful. They need the dignity and honor that standing shoulder to shoulder with the mainstream can provide. The rich don't need the labor or cultural insight of the poor. They need the boldness, the faith and the humility that come with the poverty of spirit evident in so many of our brothers and sisters on the margins.

Until we create churches and organizations where margin and mainstream are woven into a single fabric, we will not be able to dismantle the industrial complex that delights to keep us in our insular, impoverished cocoons.

Freeing Our Organizations to Become Interdependent

Creating healthy interdependence is a process for which I have few practical next steps to suggest. Each fellowship and organization has a different array of relationships in which to place themselves under mutual submission. How each guards against creating proprietary divisions of leadership and resources will vary from ministry to ministry. The larger the organization or church, the more difficult this will be, which is a motivation to keep our ministries and churches decentralized and modestly sized.

In the short-term mission world, and in the world of economic development, the best interdependence I have witnessed has been on an indi-

vidual program level. For instance, we have sent numerous campus leaders
from the United States to spend time in fellowship with leaders in local
campus ministries in Asia, Africa and Latin America. They have invested
time into getting to know each other with very little in the way of an
agenda—beyond the agenda of building a relationship. In the process they
learn about each other's assets and felt needs. It is out of this journey of
mutual discovery that leaders begin to dream about places where they
might come together to make a contribution to each other's ministries.
Programs that come of this slow and deliberate relationship building are
then co-planned and co-led. Each party makes costly investments of time
and resources—all of it without elaborately crafted contracts or a singular
leader from one country calling the shots. It is a costly, organic process that
usually ends up bearing incredible fruit and healthy interdependence.

Perhaps it is out of experiments on a smaller scale that international ministries can grow the ways in which they become living, interconnected bodies
over the long haul. We need to move beyond a representative form of governance, where agents or advocates come to an international table in order to
make certain that their interests are protected. This plays into a law of competition rather than collaboration. We need to take stock of what each party
brings into the family and employ those gifts to the benefit of the greater
fellowship. We can dream together about how our interdependence might
bring about greater outcomes than a strict, business-like partnership.

But just how do we come to understand and clarify our outcomes? How
might we define our metrics in ways that do not succumb to the superficial
counting of people or programs? To do this we will need to take a long,
hard look at how the corporate paradigm has sabotaged our understanding
of measuring organizational health.

8

FROM GROWTH TO FLOURISHING

In the world of corporate-styled capitalism, growth is king. It is the chief gauge of health and is the altar on which everything is sacrificed. But in a living organism there is a medical term for unabated growth—*cancer*.

Those who make their living in the sales world know just how unforgiving the obsession with growth and its accompanying metrics can be. If you don't make your quotas, you don't last long. Right at this moment, I have a creative, winsome and intelligent friend who, after six good years with a communications company, is getting his résumé ready because of a few months of "bad numbers." Nobody in the for-profit world is satisfied with sales staying level or, God forbid, dipping. The only acceptable direction for sales figures to go from one quarter to the next is up. The pressure is sufficiently intense to turn honest, hardworking people into swindlers willing to cook the books in order to present the appearance of upward figures in the face of downward realties. Gross sales, market share, return on investment, cost of customer acquisition, profit loss—these serve as adrenaline for the principalities of profit. Thankfully, the "triple bottom line" has gained popularity in some for-profit businesses.[1] Unfortunately, profit tends to occupy a hierarchical position above people and planet—that is to say, there is a limit to how far a for-profit business will allow social and environmental responsibility to erode profit. After all, if for-profit businesses are no longer profitable, they are no longer a for-profit business.

This worship of increase occupies the uncritically adopted worldview of our churches and nonprofits. Admittedly, there are certain kinds of growth we ought to look for in order to assess the level of health in our ministries. (More on this later.) But the sad truth is that Protestants universally seem to accept growth as the sole measure of health. This is not only true in the West. Numeric growth is the holy grail among churches and ministries around the world. We act as though the Great Commission of Christ is some sort of numbers game rather than about the reign of God over all things. The increase of Christ's government and peace defy the easy metrics of the business world, which the church often translates into number of baptisms, congregants and churches, or the size of annual budgets, staff or the number of people served through various ministries. These numbers may provide some helpful information, but they are flimsy indicators of Christ's reign. And when we succumb to measuring the mission of God solely by these metrics, we succumb to the principalities of profit and miss true signs of kingdom health.

Large churches or ministries are not promised to the faithful servant of Christ; suffering is. Success as measured by the size of one's following is not a guarantee for the obedient. Otherwise both John the Baptist and Jesus would have been considered dismal failures at the time of their deaths. To be sure, numbers are reported in Scripture. There is a whole book devoted to them. But the measures we see in Scripture, like the five thousand people fed with a few loaves and two fish (Mark 6), or the three thousand who came to faith in Acts 2, almost always point to the miraculous and mysterious work of the Spirit rather than the strategy or ingenuity of a person or ministry. We'd like to sanctify our slavery to growth by pointing to these references. But after the feeding of the five thousand in Mark 6, we encounter Mark 8, where only four thousand were fed. But we don't find Jesus and the disciples puzzling about what went wrong. From a modern perspective, a 20 percent drop in ministry should have alarmed the leadership, but this is not the case. And in Acts 4 when only two thousand additional hearers came to faith at Peter's preaching, the apostles did not call for a focus group to determine what went wrong and how to reengineer the message or conditions in order to achieve the three thousand converts they had experienced earlier. Rather than an invitation to tie the health of ministry to numbers, these records testify to the work of the Spirit, not the work of the strategist.

In 1 Chronicles 21 and 2 Samuel 24 David took a census of Israel's fighting men, and God's anger was kindled. Some scholars suggest that David was using this census in order to arouse confidence in the strength of Israel's numbers. Others say it was fodder for boasting about the political state he had built. Either way, the idea of numbering people as a way to measure kingdom success feels dubious if not outright disobedient. "I planted, Apollos watered, but God gave the growth," Paul asserts (1 Corinthians 3:6).

HANDS IN THE AIR AND BUTTS ON A PEW

In the two-thousand-year history of Christianity, tracking the number of people who show up at church or who raise their hands at an evangelistic event is a relatively new phenomenon, probably beginning sometime around the Second Great Awakening (c. 1790–1840). Japanese evangelist Kanzo Uchimura, who studied in the United States in the 1920s, said,

> Americans must count in order to see or show its value. . . . To them big churches are successful churches. . . . To win the greatest number of converts with the least expense is their constant endeavor. Statistics is their way of showing success or failure in their religion as in their commerce and politics. Numbers, numbers, oh how they value numbers![2]

One great preacher of the late 1800s was a successful evangelist by nearly any measure. For those who believe numbers to be an indicator of success, Charles Spurgeon, by preaching to around ten million people in his lifetime, must have been one of the most successful preachers of all time. If audience size is an accounting of success, then Spurgeon was more successful than Jesus and Paul put together. Still, Spurgeon was suspicious of this tendency to count conversions.

I am weary of this public bragging, this counting of unhatched chickens, this exhibition of doubtful spoils. Lay aside such numberings of the people, such idle pretense of certifying in half a minute that which will need the testing of a lifetime. Hope for the best, but in your highest excitements be reasonable. [Numbering converts is] all very well; but if they lead to idle boastings, they will grieve the Holy Spirit, and work abounding evil.[3]

Nonetheless, a fascination with counting has grown among Protestants in the last couple hundred years. Early on in the Protestant experience, baptism or membership registries were carefully recorded, but they were not generally used to assess church growth or success. These served as a public record for a variety of purposes. Somewhere in the northern European DNA of Protestantism—was it the German penchant for measurement, the Swiss tendency toward precision or the Dutch love of thrift?—we have been enamored of keeping ledgers with baptisms, marriages, births and deaths. But as a capitalist and consumerist culture began to take root in our minds, counting church attendance or baptisms has been translated into a primary measure of kingdom success.

One of America's largest online churches has created a tool for church metrics that they call, conveniently enough, Church Metrics. It helps church leaders keep tabs on the most important numbers for a congregation, like "attendance, giving, salvations, baptisms, and more." And this church knows a thing or two about counting. Their 2012 year in review is a head-spinning panoply of numbers.[4] It was so numerically inspiring I was compelled to count the number of arithmetical references in the video report. Thirty-six different statistics are paraded before viewers in the course of three minutes. Not small numbers either. For instance, more than 78 million unique devices downloaded the Bible app they produced, which logged over 38 billion minutes engaging in God's Word. Attendance at their church grew by more than 10,000 people; they baptized more than 2,400 and saw 23,000 conversions. Parts of the report felt a little like the annual report for a building and loan company:

> Your generosity and cost-effective stewardship have created financial margin for expanded kingdom investment. As a result, we've aggressively expanded our physical presence through the launch of a new campus in Broken Arrow, Oklahoma, permanent buildings in Owasso, Oklahoma and Wellington, Florida and acquisition of properties for future campuses in Jenks, Oklahoma, Moore, Oklahoma and Keller Texas.[5]

I am fairly certain that this church is contributing to the flourishing of God's kingdom. The problem is that I am not sure any of these numbers really tell me a great deal about the lasting kingdom impact of the church. I've seen several amazing Christian empires mushroom in a short period of time and then shrivel and disappear, leaving relatively little in the way of lasting signs of their existence. Jesus tells his followers that he appointed them to bear fruit that will last (John 15:16), and our fixation with measuring short-term gains at superficial levels simply means that the barrage of numbers in our annual reports are sometimes only giving us phantom signs of health.

Some scholars suggest that the largest number of items a human can see and know without guessing or physically counting is four.[6] That is, if there are five ants crawling on the table in front of a person, he or she cannot tell how many bugs are there without either counting or guessing. This seems on the low side to me, but you can do your own experiment. Take a handful of change, throw it on the floor, and without counting, spout off the number of coins on the ground. Some may be able to look at a smattering of change and know with a glance that there are eight coins, but most people would not be able to look at a birthday cake of, say, twenty-four candles and tell immediately how many there are. We are limited in comprehending very many items without some mathematical abstraction. It would be difficult for the average person to visualize one thousand gallons of water. Therefore, the meaningfulness of 78 million users downloading the church's Bible app engaging in 38 billion minutes of Scripture reading is incomprehensibly meaningless to most. I wonder if the scene of a great multitude "which no one could count" in Revelation 7 is a friendly elbow in the ribs to contemporary evangelicals who may be tempted to pull out their mobile devices and open the Church Metrics app in order to accurately measure exactly how many souls are there worshiping.

WHAT COUNTING CAN OR CAN'T TELL US

Counting does have its place in the body of Christ. I am pretty sure Jesus wants a big bride. Though the Hebrew word for "fill" can be understood as fulfill, complete or satisfy, the command to "fill the earth" is something of an indication of God's interest in having many image bearers satisfying the planet, subduing those things out of alignment with God and assuming governance. There are passages that speak of God creating "all things" and placing all things under Christ (also "You have given them dominion over the works of your hands; / you have put all things under their feet" [Psalm 8:6]). This suggests there is no area God is apathetic about. Scripture also tells us every human is important to God. Sometimes acknowledging the paucity of our Christian community in a sea of intense brokenness can wake us up to a fresh hunger for the kingdom of God. God's good reign is a beautiful thing for the whole of humanity, and God desires to restore all people to right relationships with one another, with creation and with the Creator. The mission of God is more expansive and inclusive than most of us have ability to comprehend, let alone ambition to seize.

The mission of God is more expansive and inclusive than most of us have ability to comprehend, let alone ambition to seize.

Metrics that help us understand who is or isn't in the room can be valuable. If Jesus was serious about us making disciples of *all* nations, then there is validity in asking questions about the breadth of our work. For those who carry God's passion for an entire campus, a whole neighborhood or a particular city, it is worth knowing who is not at the table. Celeste works with a community in Bangkok, Thailand, who is woefully under-represented in churches and ministries—the lady boys. These are people born male but who, often in childhood, were assigned a female gender by a parent or relative. Little is being done to reach out to or to make space for lady boys in Christian circles. Celeste struggles to find churches willing to journey with men whose female gender was mostly imposed by others and is now the only way they have to view themselves. She says that some lady boys who discover the love of Jesus and become believers at a relatively young age may in time rediscover and embrace their birth gender. But she has seen very few take this path, even after coming under Christ's redeeming love. Churches, Celeste tells me, have a fairly small window of patience. Lady boys who are faithful followers of Jesus but have been so thoroughly programmed as females that they may spend their entire lives as lady boys generally do not find a place in churches, let alone an invitation to enter into ministry. Counting the number of people in church tells us little. Identifying who is not at church is extremely valuable. So perhaps a healthy metric for churches in Bangkok could be discovered by asking, Where are the lady boys in our church community? If the redeeming and restoring power of Christ is for everyone, then we should ask who is consistently absent from our circles. This sort of assessment is helpful.

It is also true that most healthy things grow—as I have "grown" in weight I might rather suggest that healthy things can multiply. If healthy things do grow, it is not without rhythms of rest and occasional decline. In the case of InterVarsity, years of seeing no increase in the number of people involved in our chapters provoked healthy introspection. It appeared the stagnation was due, at least in part, to a lack of good training and to inconsistency in our faithful witness to the goodness of God in Christ. Time and energy spent increasing our commitment to prayer, overcoming fears and becoming more faithful to bear witness to the grace of Christ brought on a season of growth.

In these cases, paying attention to numbers has its place in the Christian faith.

A mass exodus or mass influx of people tells us something, and it may be important for us to keep track of these things so we can address the situation. But we must not be too quick to assume what growth spurts or attendance drops say about our community. One church in my town had a large bump in attendance. It turns out a church across town had a messy, divisive fallout, and many of the disgruntled members migrated to this church. In this particular case the massive growth of one church was actually an indicator of an illness in the larger community of faith. The pastor of the growing church wisely called the newcomers to a meeting. He challenged them to reconcile with the leadership of the church they had left. This pastor wanted to maintain the unity of the body as best he could and realized these disgruntled people may be carrying unhealthy expectations or postures into the growing church.

GROWING OUR EGOS

We measure ourselves and one another by such shallow calculations. I heard a story about one pastor at a conference checking the stats on attendance for the speaker's church in order to know whether to give the presenter his attention. This posture reinforces the false notion that church and mission success is tied to the charisma or effort of an individual leader who bears credit for large numbers, or the shame and responsibility for poor numbers. Looking through a handful of church leadership or church growth books, we see private ownership language referring to "my" or "your" ministry. It is a tendency handed to us from the for-profit world, to assign ownership of churches and ministries to individuals. Paul states, "So neither the one who plants nor the one who waters is anything, but only God who gives the growth" (1 Corinthians 3:7). Jesus likens the kingdom to a seed in the ground. The farmer who scatters the seed and harvests the crop is mystified at the actual "work" of transformation happening below the ground (Mark 4:26-29). The farmer does not command or coax the seed to bring forth the plant. There may be some variables under his control, but bringing life from a seed is part of the mystery and beauty of God's creation. One reason God was reluctant to give Israel a king may have been the human tendency to ascribe kingdom achievement to a person. Counting in Christian mission is so often used to celebrate our brilliance rather than God's.

Our egos freely attach themselves to things they shouldn't. I regularly fight the temptation to measure my sense of significance by the size of my "platform." How many people are reading my blog, retweeting my tweets or participating in programs I helped to build? These numbers say very little about whether I am doing what God has called me to do. Sometimes it is right to go small, to narrow our focus, to tighten our screen and choose to work with an extremely limited number of people. There are also times when it is right to work with the wide end of the funnel, to seek a broad audience and to engage as many people as possible. The problem is that my ego will always drive me toward the wide audience, even when the Spirit calls me to the narrow one. We need to be vigilant about the Spirit of God's greatest competitor, our ego. We live in a culture that pressures us to become the next Super Target when so few want to become the obscure but critical neighborhood grocery store.

In my organization, annual reporting of the size of one's campus fellowship can feed our deepest insecurities or inspire our most entrenched messianic complexes. Someone in ministry to faculty on a small liberal arts campus may be working with just a handful of professors. This person might be doing a phenomenal job in energizing faculty to invest in their students or helping them connect their research to their faith, but when it comes time to annually report the four professors he worked with this past year, it can be an effort to keep his sense of self-worth intact when a colleague working with undergraduate students is over-

We need to be vigilant about the Spirit of God's greatest competitor, our ego.

seeing a chapter of three hundred students. A part-time staff on a community college campus may have absolutely given herself away to nine students, four of whom are single mothers trying to manage a faith journey alongside their demanding studies, a dead-end part-time job and three kids. That staff worker may have been immensely successful in her campus ministry, but writing that little, single digit—9—on a form she knows will be considered in her performance review can be a depressing moment. Likewise, reporting that your ministry (there it is, that little word *your* celebrating the private ownership of ministry—even I unconsciously support this fallacy in my speech and writing) grew from forty to eighty people might go to your head. It can be a challenge to continue faithfully plugging away in one corner of a vegetable garden when your friend is working a three-hundred-acre cornfield. It takes enormous effort to hear God's voice when we have been invited to minister in an area of the kingdom that does not have much *wow* appeal. And it is equally challenging to refrain from attributing growth to ourselves when all we did was plant and water good seed, which we did not create, in good soil, which we only happened upon.

I think one of the reasons we grasp at numbers and attempt to appropriate growth to our efforts is a corrupted view of productivity. In the end, I'm not so sure God is as obsessed with productivity as we are.

I live in Wisconsin. During the wintertime, one might swear that the landscape is straight out of a dystopian novel. The death, or near death, of everything that grows happens with great regularity around here. Someone not used to it might assume the end is near. But just when we think nothing will be the same again, life returns with bravado in April and May.

The fact is that I live in a state considered part of the breadbasket of the United States. The world feeds off of the agricultural productivity of Wisconsin. We are ranked thirteenth out of fifty states for our international agricultural exports. Yet Wisconsin looks like a postapocalyptic wasteland from November to March. Most everything that comes out of the earth grinds to a frightening halt.

My point here is this: agriculturally speaking, Wisconsin is one of the most flourishing corners of the planet, and it undergoes a yearly rhythm of severe dormancy and death. In fact, I would guess that just about everything living requires regular cycles of dormancy. While it might be true that healthy things grow, healthy things also sleep. So if the kingdom of God is more like a living organism than a corporation, why do we expect our churches and ministries to experience perpetual and unhindered expansion year after year?

GOD'S UNPRODUCTIVE DESIGN

If I created a computer that shut itself down for eight hours every day, and then for the remaining sixteen hours required a fair bit of time and money to feed it the fuel it needed to run, I would be laughed out of the industry. Like most human items, computers are designed for productivity.

Psalm 121 says, "He who keeps Israel will neither slumber nor sleep." God may have voluntarily chosen to rest after the act of creation, but there is nothing in the Bible that leads me to believe God needs to sleep one-third of every day. Humans are made in God's image in some remarkable ways, but not in this one wondrous aspect. God designed us genetically to be dormant for one third of our lives. If productivity were a key value, this was a serious design flaw. But let's say that this built-in dormancy cycle gives us the ability to get three times as much work done during our waking moments. If that were the case you'd think that God would be eager for us to hop to this business of replenishing, subduing and governing with what's left of our waking hours. But this is not the case. In addition to cutting our productivity by one-third through sleep, God instituted the sabbath. Chopping one day of work out of every seven has the effect of adding another 9.5 percent of our available, waking life in unproductive periods of dormancy.

So with nearly 43 percent of our capacity for production removed by a combination of our genetic code and God's command, we should be making some serious hay with the rest of our time—quite literally, at least for Old Testament agrarian Israel. But then God issued this unusual requirement that for one year out of every seven the Israelites were to refrain from planting, cultivating and harvesting their crops. This is beginning to get ridiculous. Another 9.5 percent of their productive work lives were hamstrung by a law that necessitated one sabbatical year of rest out of every seven.

Now we're up to more than half our lives in dormancy, and I haven't even begun to calculate the time required to prepare, eat and eliminate food, not to mention the incessant need for liquids, regular washing of ourselves and our surroundings, the need to provide clothing for our bodies and shelter for our families. Couldn't we just operate on solar power and live in unadorned caves? Was it beyond God's creative capacity to design beings who did not require such onerous upkeep? Maybe with the aid of machines and the division of labor we can push basic upkeep down to only 10 percent of our life, but even so we've not yet factored in the incredibly time-consuming work inherent in social structures. Building relationships, falling in love, breaking up, miscommunicating with housemates, falling out of love, then back in love (repeat several times), reconciling with our housemates, waiting on hold with the cable company, time spent in procreation (this is not so onerous), raising kids and so forth: it's all so messy and necessitates gobs of the precious little time and energy that we could be using to produce things. When all is said and done, I estimate the time available to us for focused, uninterrupted production to be about 20 to 30 percent.

Human beings are certainly some of the least efficient organisms in the universe if our chief aim is to get stuff done for God.

> **Human beings are certainly some of the least efficient organisms in the universe if our chief aim is to get stuff done for God.**

Our genetic propensity to shut down each day, the time required to address our basic needs and our complex social structures are evidence that God did not make us with efficiency and productivity in mind. It was God's delight to make us for the sheer pleasure of it. While it may be that there is a God-shaped void in every person's heart that only Christ can fill, it also appears that there is a human-shaped void in God's heart that only we can fill. Our calling to replenish, subdue and govern cannot occupy 100 percent of our time, not even 50 percent if we take God's rest commands seriously. Our primary design may have more to do with intimacy with God and one another than with production. The obsession in most Protestants to "do," which Max Weber called the Protestant work ethic, actually runs against the grain of our design.

This is not to say that there is no beauty and godliness in work, or that we should not work hard, or that the time-consuming activity of loving God and each other is not a form of holy work. It is simply to say that in the corporate paradigm, labor for production is valued nearly as highly as profit. Production becomes the fuel burning inside the star of profit in the corporate solar system. As a result, our identity and value become entangled in what we produce. Locating our core identity in what we produce is not how we were meant to see ourselves. Pressure at our jobs is among the chief sources of stress for Americans.[7] Those in Christian ministry experience burnout as much or more than those in other fields, which indicates that the industrial complex we have constructed for our faith is failing us.[8]

We possess an innate worth to God and to all creation, even in our stillness, even in sleep or in quiet and in dormancy. "Fill the earth," God commanded. Simply living on earth has value. These realities are missed in our frenetic attempts to produce amazing numbers. I try to spend one work day each month at a Benedictine retreat center. Part of that time is devoted to lying still. I don't pray or attempt to listen to God (that comes later). Even our contemplative activities are laced with production when they hinge on striving to hear from God. There is value in simply being in God's presence without the burden of searching for a message or praying. So I simply lie there and press every thought out of my mind until all is quiet. I breathe in, "The Lord is my shepherd," I breathe out, "I shall not want." When I get to a place of complete dormancy, I open myself to the reality of God's pleasure with me even in this state of doing absolutely nothing. God loves and values me while in a posture of total inactivity.

I base some of this conviction on my own experience as a father. Infants contribute no production or labor to our communities. They are, in fact, extremely labor intensive and extremely unprofitable. They do nothing but demand time, attention and money. They are takers. Yet, I was often overwhelmed simply watching my infant son and daughters sleep. I could think of nothing more valuable than these unproductive, work-intensive babies. Why do we delight in a creature who can only cry, poop, eat and sleep? It is the divine imprint, which loves without expecting productivity in return.

I remember one of my mentors, Bill, telling me that when his daughter, Janey, was six years old she asked if she could help him in his garden. Now Bill was quite fond of his garden. It gave him tremendous pleasure to work it by himself. "I knew," Bill told me, "that if I let Janey work with me, she'd get covered in dirt, the rows would be crooked, some of the seeds would not be deep enough and others would be too deep, and the garden would not be very productive that year." Then Bill's eyes welled up with tears as he looked back on those days nearly thirty years prior, "But oh the sweet fellowship we shared in that garden!"

God is not so interested in what you can do. Your nearness matters infinitely more. Our working alongside the Creator in the garden of the cosmos, regardless of what this effort appears to produce (or not), is sweet beyond our understanding. So let's be careful in our fetish for numbers. They give us only a sliver of information in a very long and many-layered story. Numbers may tempt us to say, "Look at what our hands have done," when in fact it is God that causes the increase. They can warp our sense of worth, either inflating our egos or emasculating our self-esteem. We must anchor our value before God apart from what we produce for the industrial complex, and we must establish our identity outside of our potency to build Christian ministries or win souls or fill pews.

So where is it appropriate to measure the increase of Christ's government and his peace, and what is our part in it?

MEASURING THE KINGDOM

If we are to strive first for God's kingdom and righteousness, then what might be some signs that the kingdom is flourishing? If I look at the prophetic announcements about what it looks like for God's reign to come, and if I like to count things, then maybe I should start counting the number of weapons beat into agricultural implements and the number of blind who receive sight or the number of dead people raised in Jesus' name. When John the Baptist sent some of his disciples to ask Jesus whether he was the real deal or not, Jesus did not reply with numbers of baptisms or followers: "Go and tell John what you hear and see: the blind receive their sight, the lame walk, the lepers are cleansed, the deaf hear, the dead are raised, and the poor have good news brought to them" (Matthew 11:4-5). These are some of the prophetic indicators that God's reign has come to earth.

Every church or ministry has only a slice of the whole vision for kingdom flourishing. Recognizing the particular charism on our lives or ministries or churches is critical. Acknowledging that we play a small part and that we desperately depend on others will keep us from arrogance. Too often individual churches or ministries have tried to take it all on. The impossibility of replenishing, subduing and governing on my own is an invitation to solidarity, community and dependence on God. Those working to shut down brothels may not be able to provide aftercare. However, they are foolish if they act on their own without adequate partnership with those bearing the aftercare charism. They must listen to missionaries and social workers living alongside of and serving those in the sex industry. They will have to work closely with secular forces in the judicial system and law enforcement. To effect lasting change in an area rife with sex tourism, dozens of different communities may need to work together toward a vision of kingdom flourishing, each understanding their particular role and honoring the roles others must play. These relationships are themselves a sign of God's reign and the excellence of God's design.

Once we understand the particular mantle carried by the ministry we are involved with, then meaningful metrics associated with that particular mantle will be identified. Perhaps one will have a church-planting focus, in which not only the number of churches but a series of other indicators help to reveal just how vibrant and functional each new church may be. This might include the number of baptisms or number of people involved, but likely it will need to involve evaluating individual and community life over a period of time: things like levels of stress ("my yoke is easy, and my burden is light" [Matthew 11:30]), economic sufficiency ("There was not a needy person among them" [Acts 4:34]) and quality of life ("I came that they may have life, and have it abundantly" [John 10:10]). These qualities may be a challenge to quantify, but they are the sorts of signs that give a clearer picture of the health of a church plant. The number of churches or people involved tells us very little.

Any church-planting mission working in communities where there is poverty, domestic abuse, drug use, materialism, violence, poor sanitation, racism or any variety of obstructions to the vision of God for the earth must work in partnership with others in order to see kingdom flourishing. The mere presence of believers or a church is not enough. A Pauline approach to mission is shortsighted without the ministry of James, who addressed an entirely different set of issues critical to God's kingdom righteousness, or Barnabas, who accomplished similar church-planting outcomes as Paul but using a different set of values in his mission. No one ministry can do it all, which is why the metaphor of a body is important. Most view this metaphor in the context of a solitary local church or ministry. We want the individuals in our church and our ministries to see themselves as connected to other individuals performing different roles. But the body imagery is also a vision for Beloved Communities within the universal church, which is larger than any one mission community. The churches in Paul's day worked together with various missionary bands to care for one another and establish the early foundations of the kingdom of God.

Once there is a solid sense of a church's or ministry's calling, strengths and limitations, along with a few health indicators for the small patch of God's garden it works in, and once a ministry has constructed intentional bridges to people and organizations who are working toward a vision of shalom (some of whom may be secular governing authorities who do not share our faith but contribute to kingdom justice nonetheless), then there may be some common signs and numbers that will build a more complete picture of whether we are contributing to God's vision for us to replenish, subdue and govern, without becoming mired in one-dimensional and superficial metrics.

FREEING FLOURISHING FROM OUR ADDICTION TO GROWTH

I have observed some helpful indicators that are better gauges of a flourishing kingdom than the superficial counting handed us by the corporate paradigm.

Our own spiritual maturity. One of the first things we need to evaluate is how we and our colaborers are growing in spiritual maturity. We can only export what we grow domestically. We can't grow others in their love for God if we aren't actively growing in love for God ourselves. So one way to help insure that we are contributing to the flourishing of God's kingdom is by attending to our own flourishing. So much of our fruitfulness is lost to burnout. This is why a key sign of the kingdom is the spiritual flourishing of God's people, in which we need to evaluate, measure and spur each other along. In every InterVarsity job description, for each of the fifteen hundred staff—whether office workers or field workers—we have as a common responsibility our own discipleship. Therefore, in the performance reviews I give, I like to evaluate the ways in which each coworker that I supervise is maturing as a disciple. Within Catholic orders, God's mission inside the missionary is as critical as God's mission through the missionary.

This is not easy to accomplish when we reduce missionaries to an employee and are concerned mainly with their measurable output. The employee is valued by the corporate-styled mission only inasmuch as they provide a bona fide business outcome. Sanctification of the missionary should be a legitimate outcome of the mission. In the typical 501c3 structure, we are limited in the ways we can employ someone who, because of a physical, emotional or spiritual setback, can no longer perform functions tied to businesslike ministry outcomes. This is why many nonprofit structural paradigms set up by the government push us toward a business model. Our own spiritual growth needs to be woven into the fabric of our organization's purpose and mission.

Rhythms of dormancy. I believe that our lives, as well as the missions and churches we participate in, need regular times of rest and lying fallow. If sabbaticals are given, often it is only for field workers. Most clergy don't even take all their vacation time let alone take a sabbatical. Sabbaticals are healthy for all of us, and thoughtful mission organizations (as well as healthy businesses, for that matter) will give regular sabbaticals to their workers. This is not the same as vacation time, which is also needed. One of my bosses worked with me to develop a six-month sabbatical, which I took in 2010. "I don't believe in sabbaticals that are exclusively focused on rest," he told me. "If you are not working in a sustainable way, a sabbatical to recover from burnout is not the long-term solution." I respected that viewpoint. I attempt to work in a sustainable way, so I can create sabbaticals focused on developing deeper self-awareness and components of my spirituality that are difficult to pursue while working full time. Each of us needs to grow our understanding of our identity outside of our work environment. We need to continually discover who we are becoming. We need extended time to step out of our vocation to process where we've been and look at the world through different lenses. Whether working in an exclusively administrative role as an executive leader or working in the field, we need extended times of disengagement to remain healthy.

I think this is true for our organizations as well. Most ministries are more like living organisms than machines. Seasons of slowing down, plateau or even of fallow are to be expected and planned for. The simpler the organizational structure, the easier this will be to build in seasons of rest. Each area must be given the possibility of slowing down significantly—if not winding down completely for a season. It is important to build into our plans regular intervals when the breathing and heart rate of our operations significantly decelerates. What does rest look like for the various aspects of our ministry? If we want our ministries to produce lasting fruit, we must discover the right rhythms of dormancy, discern when and how often they should occur, synchronize this slowdown with other areas, and build it into our planning cycles.

Discipleship as mission. Jesus' command was not to go and make converts or build churches or to gather attendees. It was to go and make disciples and to teach the nations to obey the way of life he imparted. That's why Jesus' disciples were initially called followers of "the Way." They were marked by a lifestyle. This requires people encountering the resurrected person of Christ, coming under his leadership and gathering in community with others who are also working out their faith. But that is not an end in itself; nor does it automatically produce serious students of Jesus. When the way we live as Christians becomes central to understanding kingdom metrics, we will experience lasting fruit. The task of replenishing, subduing and governing can only be accomplished as we expand our ability to love well, to die to ourselves, and learn to hear and obey God's voice. How do we measure someone's growth in the area of love? What about their willingness to die to self or to discern God's voice? These belie the simple, external growth metrics born of a corporate paradigm.

Brian was a student sent on one of our short-term trips to China. Each student is assigned a Chinese university student counterpart. Brian's counterpart, Jay (a pseudonym), had gotten into the program because his well-connected dad thought his son would benefit by participating in this program with American students. Jay actually had no interest in the program. He ditched Brian whenever he could to hang out with his friends off campus. With great disappointment Brian would hear stories of how his teammates were hitting it off with their counterparts. Jay could be relatively cruel to Brian and callous to the fact that Brian had saved his money, traveled thousands of miles and dreamed all year about the Chinese friend he would make. Still, Brian hung in there, loving Jay as best he knew how. When the program came to an end and Jay promised to see Brian off at the train station, Brian waited eagerly to say goodbye and give Jay a parting gift. As the train pulled away with no sign of Jay, Brian began to weep. "I knew in that moment," Brian said, "that I had truly learned to love."

Brian learned to die to his own desires. He learned to hear and obey God's call to keep reaching out unconditionally. And he learned to grow in his affection for someone who treated him poorly. These qualities will serve Brian for the rest of his life, but it is hard to put into a statistic. The increase of a severe and practical love in the lives of believers is the kind of thing we should be looking for to assess the health of our churches and organizations.

> The increase of a severe and practical love in the lives of believers is the kind of thing we should be looking for to assess the health of our churches and organizations.

Measuring for the long haul. Unless we build into our mission the kind of steady evaluation that looks twenty to thirty years down the road, we are catering to a short-term vision of health born of the book-cooking, short-term accounting inherited from a corporate worldview that panders to what investors want to hear. Many of our ministries try to furnish donors with immediate results. But quick results are unsustainable. They often burn through our staff and our resources just to achieve a big bang. It may not be possible to track everyone who has touched or been touched by our ministry over decades, but certainly there are a small number of people or communities we have walked with over a long period who can help us estimate our impact. Longitudinal study is slow and painful work. It can be as dreaded as a colonoscopy, requiring a willingness to uncover the truth of just how sick we may be deep inside those unseen places. But these measures may be a truer indication of flourishing than our penchant for short-term gains.

Financial accountability. As ruthless as I appear to have been on the fact that money occupies too much space in our lives and our ministries, I actually think it is important to carefully measure how we handle it. Carefully monitoring our use of money is valuable since money is a form of power, and all forms of power are easily corrupted. Choosing the lean approach is almost always more sustainable than building cash-hungry behemoths.

IS THE BRIDE READY?

The end of the book of Revelation is one picture of the kingdom of God. In chapter 19 the marriage of the Lamb is announced because "his bride has made herself ready" (Revelation 19:7). What follows in Revelation 21–22 is a stunning picture of life as it was meant to be, without the curse of sin and death. Sorrow has ceased, tears are no more, and the community of the Trinity lives in the midst of humanity. Rather than humans going to heaven, a city, the new Jerusalem, is located on earth. A place whose gates are always open, for this city needs no police force, no protection. National leaders and citizens bring the glorious creations, discoveries and goodness of their countries into this place, and national wounds are healed.

What might we expect to see on the nearer side of Revelation 21–22? This is not clear. What is clear is that we are to seek first the kingdom described in those passages and the justice that accompanies it. We are to pray for this kingdom to come on earth and to be made real here. The extent and outcome of our efforts cannot be counted by the easy metrics of the corporate mindset. I have no problem with measuring the increase of Christ's government and peace, but we must be careful not to become enthralled with the size of our churches and ministries as the chief indicator of that increase.

Growth is not all it is cracked up to be. An obsession with numeric expansion tempts the ego, invites comparison, robs us of the necessity of becoming interdependent with others, derails sabbath, denies our God-given limitations, and can lead to a focus on building empires rather than on kingdom flourishing. One of the surest ways to keep us grounded on the power of God is to shed our egos, embrace our limitations, tie our churches and organizations to each other, and learn to look for signs of flourishing over the long haul.

EPILOGUE

Putting Our Shoulders to the Donkey Cart

The heat of Cairo in the summer can be unforgiving. When added to the smells in the garbage village, zeal melts into lethargy. I remember climbing the hill inside this garbage collectors' community to the Coptic Christian monastery where my family lived with a team of American college students. Just in front of me, a single donkey suffered under an impossible load of refuse, struggling to reach the crest of the only paved road in the community. Unkempt hooves curled upward, patches of fur were missing from the beast, and it slipped and fell to its front knees once or twice, all the while I followed with my daughter, Hannah, who was twelve at the time. Atop the cart piled with garbage, the donkey cart driver urged the animal forward under the motivation of a whip. Hannah looked at me with pleading eyes as the tormented donkey struggled up the hill. As much as I felt sorry for myself, panting up the hill in 110 degree heat, I began to have compassion for the donkey. *Why?* I wondered. *What could I do anyway? I cannot relieve the donkey's plight any more than I can relieve my own misery climbing this insufferable hill.*

Step by sweaty step we press on. My conscience and my daughter continue to trouble me. Finally, I give in to my unreasonable instinct. Without a glance backward from the donkey-cart driver (nor, do I guess, much noticeable relief for the donkey) I shoulder the back of the garbage cart and begin to push. *What good is it*, I wondered, *to add to my suffering only to give some inconsequential relief to this creature without even the benefit of the owner's thanks?* In fact it may have been that this Egyptian donkey cart driver would have considered me an enemy. He may have preferred I keep my hands off his cart. Still I kept pushing the stinking cart of rubbish up the hill until we reached the summit.

At the top, Hannah and I turned right, toward the monastery, and the donkey and his driver turned left, down a rubbish-strewn dirt road. There, sitting in his usual perch outside the butcher shop, was Romany. He was waiting for enough business to justify another pig slaughter. Every day we stepped through the blood and entrails that flow down in little rivulets from the hill outside Romany's shop. Romany is among those residents of the Zabbaleen, Egyptian Arabic for "Garbage People." They hold to the ancient Coptic Christian faith, delivered to Egypt, or so it is thought, from the Gospel writer Mark in the first century. Romany had been a good friend to me and our team since our arrival in the garbage village.

As I passed, Romany said three words to me I have never forgotten. Indeed, what he said to me has changed my life.

He said, quite matter-of-factly, "God saw that."

"God saw that." Those words have reverberated through my soul over these more than ten years since. I was not aware of Romany's watchful eye from his post atop the hill. As far as I was concerned, there was no one whose favor I would curry by pushing that blessed wagon of garbage, except perhaps my daughter, whose consideration of her father would, regardless of my service that day, fluctuate up and down through her teenage years. Romany wanted to remind me that to serve the suffering, the marginalized, the invisible, even beasts of burden counts for something in God's kingdom. There was something about watching an American man trying to relieve the load of a Middle Eastern, garbage-toting donkey that must have struck Romany. Perhaps Romany knew Exodus 23:5, a verse I was unaware of until discovering it as I finished this manuscript: "If you see that the donkey of someone who hates you has collapsed under its load, do not walk by. Instead, stop and help" (NLT).

Romany's encouragement has inspired me.

A faithful and yet nearly invisible form of Christian mission has been taking place for millennia on the backs of slaves of the empire. It has been advanced by people from the margins working quietly among their forgotten neighbors. Meanwhile the Christian-Industrial Complex has ballooned in size, but not in effectiveness. We have erected massive structures accessible only by middle-class and rich missionaries, while absorbing into our bloated organizations poorer, local coworkers who are, in the words of the mission agency that sent Betsey Stockton, "regarded and treated neither as equals nor servants."

This book represents an attempt to describe the mainstream Protestant mission world I find myself in—one born of a corporate, culturally white, individualist paradigm. This paradigm has achieved cultural dominance over most every human construct—political, economic and religious. This book is also an attempt to describe another world, a world which operates outside the camp, where Christ was crucified. This is a world where prisoners and prostitutes, outcasts and oppressed occupy the seats of honor. These are Christianity's new architects. They are the experts at the center of God's kingdom, and they live and work at the fulcrum of the twenty-first-century church. We would be foolish not to invite them to assist us in a process of deconstructing the industrial complex and reconstructing the ancient, lighter form of church and mission.

It is time for the Protestant church and its mission to overturn the tables of the corporate worldview that has held our imaginations hostage. It is time to reenvision a mission designed for the twenty-first century. And while new structures and new workers from the margins will certainly have their own liabilities and cultural blinders, they must become co-creators of a new season of mission.

ACKNOWLEDGMENTS

After reading through the manuscript of this book in order to offer me feedback, one of my friends asked, "Did you take a sabbatical to write this?" It was at that moment that I appreciated the price my family, particularly my wife Janine, paid for the writing of this book. I wrote *Overturning Tables* while working full time. In the evenings and on weekends I would plant myself at one corner of the living room couch and bang away at the keyboard for hours. Janine, Hannah, Philip and Laura, thanks for granting me the space to research and write this book. It is a tribute to your generosity. I have dedicated this volume to my son, Philip, who is a lover of story and the ways in which story can be told. I trust the stories told in this book will carry well the truths behind them.

To those whose stories I tell in these pages, I am grateful for the alternative vision of church and mission that you live. Philip and Beauty Ndoro, Efren and Becky Roxas, Jean-Luc and Shabrae Krieg, Joshua Palma, Dave Bookless, Nigel and Jesse Paul, my New Friars and IFES friends, and University Christian Church. Thank you for your faithfulness to God. Your living alternative to the corporate-shaped world in which we live is inspiring. I hope the words in this book bring you honor and bring God glory.

My wife, Janine, and colleague Gary Nauman provided some illustrations for the stories told here. Thanks for bringing to life these pages with your art.

The team of men and women whom I have had the privilege of leading stood alongside me as we have together questioned the status quo and experimented with different ways of thinking about and executing mission. Amber Nelson, Haley Compean, Helyn Luisi-Mills, Jill Feldkamp, Josh Harper, Katye Crawford, Lauren Dueck, Marissa Newman and Tom Sharp, thanks for your patience, encouragement, willingness to push back and willingness to push ahead as we've wrestled together over some of the concepts in this book.

Finally, in an act of either profound wisdom or immense folly I sent a draft of this manuscript out to people who are smarter than me. More than a dozen inundated me with helpful and detailed responses, sharpening this work and broadening my thinking. Thanks must finally go to the sea of people who took the time and the care to critique, affirm, challenge, rip to shreds or buttress this work. I took your words seriously and hope you see the results of your wisdom. I hesitate to list you all for fear I will miss someone or that you will not want your name associated with this book! Still, in addition to those mentioned above, credit must be given where credit is due: Lisa Rieck, Randy White, Bob Grahmann, Tom Lin, Bruce Hansen, John Hayes, Chris Heuertz, Wes Markofski, Alexia Salvatierra, Ananda Kumar, Paul Borthwick, Vinoth Ramachandra, Diana Collymore, Darren Prince, Steve Moore, Becky Stephen, Richard Coleman, Jack Voelkel, Matt Prichard, Eric Robinson and, of course, the prince of editors, Dave Zimmerman. Your input has not only impacted the book but has challenged my thinking and deepened my spiritual journey.

NOTES

PROLOGUE: DRIVING THE MARKET OUT OF CHRISTIAN MISSION

[1]David Horsey, "Pope Francis Startles Rush Limbaugh with Critique of Capitalism," *Los Angeles Times*, December 17, 2013, http://articles.latimes.com/2013/dec/17/nation/la-na-tt-pope-startles-rush-20131217.

[2]Pope Francis I, *Apostolic Exhortation Evangelii Gaudium of the Holy Father Francis to the Bishops, Clergy, Consecrated Persons and the Lay Faithful on the Proclamation of the Gospel in Today's World* (Vatican City: Vatican Press, 2013), p. 46.

[3]Harold W. Hoehner, *Herod Antipas: A Contemporary of Jesus Christ* (Grand Rapids: Zondervan, 1972), p. 70.

[4]Flavius Josephus, *Jewish Antiquities* bk. 18, chap. 5.2. Available at www.gutenberg.org/files/2848/2848-h.htm.

[5]Economic and spiritual integration was not just a Jewish reality. This was true in Roman society as well. For instance, in Acts 19 the silversmiths start a riot due to the economic *and* religious implications of people abandoning the goddess Artemis and turning to Christ: "There is danger not only that our trade will lose its good name, but also that the temple of the great goddess Artemis will be discredited; and the goddess herself, who is worshiped throughout the province of Asia and the world, will be robbed of her divine majesty" (Acts 19:26-27).

[6]For more, see *The Politics of Jesus* by John Howard Yoder (2nd ed. [Grand Rapids: Eerdmans, 1994]), and *Binding the Strong Man: A Political Reading of Mark's Story of Jesus* by Ched Myers (Maryknoll, NY: Orbis, 1988).

[7]The baptism of John (Matthew 3:1-17; Mark 1:1-11; Luke 3:1-22; John 1:15-34); the feeding of five thousand (Matthew 14:13-21; Mark 6:30-44; Luke 9:10-17; John 6:1-15); Peter's profession of faith (Matthew 16:13-19; Mark 8:27-29; Luke 9:18-20; John 6:66-71); and Jesus' anointing by Mary (Matthew 26:6-13; Mark 14:3-9; Luke 7:36-50; John 12:1-11).

[8]John separates the triumphal entry (John 12:12-19) from the clearing of the temple (John 2:13-17) placing the latter at the front of Jesus' ministry. Some resolve this tension by suggesting that Jesus cleared the temple on two occasions.

[9]Neill Q. Hamilton, "Temple Cleansing and Temple Bank," *Journal of Biblical Literature* 83, no. 4 (December 1964): 370-71.

[10]Hoehner, *Herod Antipas*, p. 49.

[11]Joachim Jeremias, *Jerusalem in the Time of Jesus: An Investigation into Economic and Social Conditions During the New Testament Period*, trans. F. H. Cave and C. H. Cave (Minneapolis: Fortress, 1969), pp. 33-34.

[12]Ibid., p. 97.

[13]Ibid., p. 98.

[14]Ched Myers, *Binding the Strong Man: A Political Reading of Mark's Story of Jesus* (Maryknoll, NY: Orbis, 2008), p. 300.

[15]See "Military-Industrial Complex Speech," given by Dwight D. Eisenhower, available in *Public Papers of the Presidents, Dwight D. Eisenhower* (Washington, DC: United States Government Printing Office, 1960,), pp. 1035-40, available online at http://coursesa.matrix.msu.edu/~hst306/documents/indust.html.

[16]Derek Thompson, "The World's 85 Richest People Are as Wealthy as the Poorest 3 Billion," *Atlantic*, January 21, 2014, www.theatlantic.com/business/archive/2014/01/the-worlds-85-richest-people-are-as-wealthy-as-the-poorest-3-billion/283206.

[17]Erin Roach, "Ethnic Leaders Affirm Value of Southern Baptist Diversity," posted June 18, 2013, on Baptist Press website, www.bpnews.net/bpnews.asp?id=40558. (Note: Of course every church is "ethnic in some shape, form or fashion." This statement was made by a white person for whom "ethnic" means not white.)

[18]"More Southern Baptists from Ethnic Minorities Needed in Global Missions," by staff, posted March 19, 2013, at www.commissionstories.com/americas/stories/view/more-southern-baptists-from-ethnic-minorities-needed-in-global-missions.

[19]"Most Children Younger Than Age 1 Are Minorities, Census Bureau Reports," May 17, 2012, US Census Bureau, www.census.gov/newsroom/releases/archives/population/cb12-90.html.

[20]Hope Yen, "Census: White Majority in U.S. Gone by 2043," June 13, 2013, Associated Press, as reported on NBC News, http://usnews.nbcnews.com/_news/2013/06/13/18934111-census-white-majority-in-us-gone-by-2043?lite.

[21]Even before I entered ministry, women in leadership came onto the agenda of the 1979 session of the Evangelical Foreign Mission Association. But for the most part, unless the topic is missionary wives, prayer, children or reaching Muslim women, there has been very little room for women to teach up front or enter senior positions.

And in terms of top-tier leadership positions, there are four female chief executives among the 150-plus sending structures represented in one major conglomerate Protestant missions entity. (As of April 2012, a woman was at the helm of Camino Global Canada—formerly CAM International of Canada—Vision Synergy, Childspring International and Brethren in Christ World Missions.)

Even the Lausanne movement, which has done a remarkable job of promoting majority world leaders into its ranks, has a board of directors that is 75 percent male, and there are no women among those who comprise Lausanne's International deputy directors and senior advisor leadership roles. Though there is a long history of patriarchal worldviews in Christian mission to overcome, and theological debate among some on the role of women, I have witnessed a weighty acknowledgment of the need for more women in leadership accompanied by little discernible movement on that score.

[22]See "Corporation," *Wikipedia.com*, http://en.wikipedia.org/wiki/Corporation.

[23]"Triple Bottom Line: It Consists of Three Ps: Profit, People and Planet," *Economist*, November 17, 2009, www.economist.com/node/14301663.

[24]Robert Woodberry, "The Missionary Roots of Liberal Democracy," *American Political Science Review* 106, no. 2 (May 2012).

[25]See Andrea Palpant Dilley, "The World the Missionaries Made," *Christianity Today*, January–February 2014, pp. 34-41.

CHAPTER 1: A TALE OF TWO MISSIONS

[1]Courtney Anderson, *To the Golden Shore: The Life of Adoniram Judson* (Valley Forge, PA: Judson Press, 1987), p. 67.

[2]Fred Field Goodsell, *You Shall Be My Witnesses: An Interpretation of the History of the American Board (1810-1960)* (Boston: American Board of Commissioners for Foreign Mission, 1959), p. 216.

[3]E. C. Tracy, *Memoir of the Life of Jeremiah Evarts: Late Corresponding Secretary of the American Board of Commissioners for Foreign Mission* (Boston: Crocker & Brewster, 1845), p. 107.

[4]The British recruited the slaves of Patriot masters with the promise of freedom. George Washington used the same tactic to bolster his ranks, though sadly many were sent back to their masters at the end of the war. During the chaos of the Revolutionary War, many black slaves escaped or joined the British. As a result, tens of thousands of slaves were freed, fled, joined the British soldiers or were evacuated at the end of the war.

[5]Albert J. Raboteau, *Slave Religion: The "Invisible Institution" in the Antebellum South* (New York: Oxford University Press, 2004), p. 141.

[6]E. A. Holmes, "George Liele: Negro Slavery's Prophet of Deliverance," *Baptist Quarterly* 20 (1963–1964): 350.

[7]Ibid., p. 349.

[8]Daniel L. Akin, *Ten Who Changed the World* (Nashville: B & H Books, 2012), p. 89.

[9]Holmes, "George Liele," p. 351.

[10]Hmar Sangkhuma, quoted in Rosie Murry-West, "Indian Tribe Sends a Missionary to Tackle Spiritual Void in Wales," *Telegraph*, March 6, 2006, www.telegraph.co.uk/news/uknews/1512204/Indian-tribe-sends-a-missionary-to-tackle-spiritual-void-in-Wales.html.

[11]"Christianity in Its Global Context: 1970-2020: Society, Religion and Mission," Center for the Study of Global Christianity, Gordon Conwell Theological Seminary, June 2013.

[12]These shifts recognize missionaries beyond the evangelical Protestant tradition. Thus the highest sending countries in 1970, Italy and Belgium (which sent 4,406 and 1,048 missionaries per million Christians respectively) reflect Catholic missions, while the explosive growth of missionaries from South Africa over this forty-year period is due to the remarkable rise of African independent churches.

[13]"'Nones' on the Rise," Pew Research: Religion and Public Life Project, October 9, 2012, www.pewforum.org/Unaffiliated/nones-on-the-rise-preface.aspx.

CHAPTER 2: FROM CORPORATION TO LOCALLY OWNED

[1]Leah S. Marcus, Janel Meuller and Mary Beth Rose, eds., *Elizabeth I: Collected Works* (Chicago: University of Chicago Press, 2000), p. 313.

[2]Susan Ronald, *The Pirate Queen: Queen Elizabeth I, Her Pirate Adventurers, and the Dawn of Empire* (New York: HarperCollins, 2007), p. 90.

[3]John W. Cowart, *Crackers and Carpetbaggers: Moments in the History of Jacksonville, Florida* (Raleigh, NC: Lulu Press, 2005), pp. 18-19.

[4]It is worth noting that many Protestants, especially missionaries, were vocal abolitionists and sometimes found themselves at odds with the capitalistic ventures that carried them abroad.

[5]Max Weber, *The Protestant Ethic and the Spirit of Capitalism*, trans. Talcott Parsons (Mineola, NY: Dover Publications, 2003), p. 17.

[6]Martin Luther, "On Trading and Usery," *The Works of Martin Luther* 4 (Philadelphia: A. J. Holman, 1915), www.godrules.net/library/luther/NEW1luther_d3. In an interesting paradox, the website where I obtained this quote was plastered with ads for Bank of America and online lenders offering fast loans for those with bad credit—at least on the days I've visited the site. Because Luther's text is littered

with financial language, the programs that generate the ads have populated the page with predatory lending offers. I could just about hear Luther rolling over in his grave.

[7]Ibid.

[8]For example, the salaries of employees at Samaritan's Purse, a Christian aid organization, averaged $25,000 per year while its chief executive officer, Franklin Graham, made over $600,000. Focus on the Family employees averaged $37,000 in salaries while president and CEO Jim Daly made well over $200,000, and many of their executive officers made around $150,000. These examples may not be typical of nonprofits and missionary organizations but are illustrative of the point. Few have raised objections over Christian ministries with such income disparities. (See average salaries of various Christian ministries at careerbliss.com, then explore salaries of their chief officers at Charitynavigator.org.)

[9]Sadly, some of the early twenty-first-century corporate scandals involved lucratively profitable companies with devoted believers at the helm (e.g., Philip Anschutz of QWest as well as executives of Enron). More to the point, many Christians would not raise an eyebrow over businesses that manipulate material desire (otherwise known as covetousness), push prices to their upper-most limit and depress wages to their lowest limit in order to maximize profit for investors and executives, regardless of challenges it might create for low-wage workers, the environment or locally owned small businesses in the community.

[10]R. H. Tawney, *Religion and the Rise of Capitalism: A Historical Study* (Gloucester, MA: Harcourt, Brace, 1926), pp. 10-11.

[11]As suggested in the introduction, Protestant history has often ignored the contributions of earlier, non-white or non-English-speaking missionaries.

[12]Timothy Tennent, *Invitation to World Missions: A Trinitarian Missiology for the Twenty-first Century* (Grand Rapids: Kregel Academic, 2010), p. 261.

[13]Orlando E. Costas, *Christ Outside the Gate: Mission Beyond Christendom* (Eugene, OR: Wipf & Stock, 1982), p. 59.

[14]David Bosch, *Transforming Mission: Paradigm Shifts in Theology of Mission* (Maryknoll, NY: Orbis, 1991), p. 227.

[15]Ibid., p. 228.

[16]Costas, *Christ Outside the Gate*, p. 60.

[17]Ibid.

[18][Annie Laurie Baird], "The Relation of the Wives of Missionaries to Mission Work," *Korean Repository* 2 (November 1885): 417, quoted in, Dae Young Ryu, "Understanding Early American Missionaries in Korea (1884–1910): Capitalist Middle-

Class Values and the Weber Thesis," *Archives de sciences sociales des religions*, January-March 2001.

[19]Ryu, "Understanding Early American Missionaries in Korea."

[20]*Consular Reports: Commerce, Manufacturers, Etc.* vol. 57, nos. 212, 213, 214, 215 (May-August 1898): 570. Available at http://books.google.com/books?id=HR9JAQAAI AAJ&printsec=frontcover&source=gbs_ge_summary_r&ead=0#v+onepage &q&f=false.

[21]Eighty-First Annual Report of the American Board of Commissioners for Foreign Missions, 1893, Boston, p. 5.

[22]The Korean mission of the various Presbyterian bodies in the United States experienced enormous success in bringing the gospel to Korea. However, some may argue that a truly indigenous Korean expression of Christianity did not flow out of this mission, rather a heavily Americanized version of church and mission emerged.

[23]Lindsay Brown, *Shining Like Stars: The Power of the Gospel in the World's Universities* (Nottingham, UK: Inter-Varsity Press, 2006), p. 29.

[24]Ibid., pp. 34-35.

Chapter 3: From Profits to Prophets

[1]Josiah Strong, *Our Country: Its Possible Future and Its Present Crisis* (New York: Baker & Taylor, 1891), p. 181.

[2]James Hudnut-Beumler, *In Pursuit of the Almighty's Dollar: A History of Money and American Protestantism* (Chapel Hill: University of North Carolina Press, 2007), p. 138.

[3]Simon Coleman, *The Globalisation of Charismatic Christianity: Spreading the Gospel of Prosperity* (Cambridge: Cambridge University Press, 2000), p. 41.

[4]The quotes in the next few paragraphs are from personal interactions and correspondence between the author and Joshua Palma.

[5]Robert F. Kennedy, University of Kansas, March 18, 1968. Available at www.jfk library.org/research/Research-Aids/Ready-Reference/RFK-Speeches/Remarks-of -Robert-F-Kennedy-at-the-University-of-Kansas-March-18-1968.aspx.

[6]See Richard Wilkinson and Kate Pickett, "The Spirit Level: Why Greater Equality Makes Societies Stronger," Tantor Audio, accessed on September 2, 2013, www.tantor .com/Extras/B0505_SpiritLevel/B0505_SpiritLevel_PDF_1.pdf; and Karen Rowlingson, "Does Income Inequality Cause Health and Social Problems?" Joseph Rowntree Foundation, September 2011, www.jrf.org.uk/sites/files/jrf/inequality -income-social-problems-full.pdf.

[7]David Korten, *When Corporations Rule the World* (Bloomfield, CT: Kumarian Press, 1995), p. 38.

[8]John Medaille, *The Vocation of Business: Social Justice in the Marketplace* (New York: Continuum, 2007), p. 37.

[9]Some are using the term "community benefit organization" for this very reason.

[10]Jonathan Bonk, *Missions And Money: Affluence as a Missionary Problem . . . Revisited* (Maryknoll, NY: Orbis, 2007).

[11]Tracy McVeigh, "One in Five Women Is a Shopaholic," *London Observer,* November 26, 2000.

[12]Andy Crouch, *Playing God: Redeeming the Gift of Power* (Downers Grove, IL: IVP Books, 2013), pp. 55-56.

[13]Matthew 5:27-32; 15:18-20; 19:3-9; Mark 7:20-23; 10:2-12; Luke 16:18; John 8:3-11.

[14]Matthew 4:8-10; 6:1-4, 19-21, 24-34; 10:8-10; 13:22; 15:17-20; 16:24-26; 19:16-26; 21:12-13; 25:31-46; Mark 4:18-19; 6:6-12; 7:17-23; 8:34-38; 10:17-27; 11:15-17; 12:41-44; Luke 6:20, 24, 29-31; 8:14; 9:3-6, 25; 10:3-12; 12:15-21, 22-34; 14:33; 16:13, 19-31; 18:18-30; 19:1-10, 45-46; 21:1-4; John 2:16; 6:26-27.

[15]1 Clement 55:2, in *The Apostolic Fathers: S. Clement of Rome. A Revised Text*, ed. J. B. Lightfoot and J. R. Harmer (New York: Macmillan, 1898).

[16]*Didascalia Apostolarum* 2.5, in R. Hugh Connolly, *Didascalia Apostolorum* (Oxford: Clarendon Press, 1929), www.bombaxo.com/didascalia.html.

[17]Ibid., 2.58.

[18]"How IMB Missions Is Funded," IMB, accessed January 24, 2014, www.imb.org/main/give/page.asp?StoryID=4426&LanguageID=1709.

[19]"Understanding Missionary Support," EFCA, accessed January 24, 2014, http://go.efca.org/resources/document/understanding-missionary-support.

[20]Paul Borthwick, *Western Christians in Global Mission: What's the Role of the North American Church?* (Downers Grove, IL: InterVarsity Press, 2012), p. 94.

[21]For more on hyperinflation in Zimbabwe and its causes, see "Hyperinflation in Zimbabwe," *Wikipedia.com*, http://en.wikipedia.org/wiki/Hyperinflation_in_Zimbabwe.

[22]Jean-Luc Krieg, "Transforming Cities: Addressing the Greatest Challenges of the 21st Century—It's Theory and Praxis," *ConeXión Mosaico*, July 2011.

[23]Richard Kersley and Michael O'Sullivan, "Global Wealth Reaches New All-Time High," Credit Suisse Research Institute, September 10, 2013, https://www.credit-suisse.com/ch/en/news-and-expertise/topics/wealth.article.html/article/pwp/news-and-expertise/2013/10/en/global-wealth-reaches-new-all-time-high.html.

CHAPTER 4: FROM CONVERT TO COSMOS

[1]Brad Gregory, *The Unintended Reformation: How a Religious Revolution Secularized Society* (Cambridge, MA, Belknap Press, 2012), p. 237.

[2]Ibid., p. 242.

[3]The medieval Catholic practice of giving money to the church for some spiritual good, such as a shortened stint in purgatory.

[4]See Scot McKnight, *The King Jesus Gospel* (Grand Rapids: Zondervan, 2011).

[5]James Hudnut-Beumler, *In Pursuit of the Almighty's Dollar: A History of Money and American Protestantism* (Chapel Hill: University of North Carolina Press, 2007), p. 98.

[6]Tim Reid, "Banks Foreclosing on Churches in Record Numbers," Reuters, March 9, 2012, www.reuters.com/article/2012/03/09/us-usa-housing-churches-idUSBRE 82803120120309.

[7]For more on this, see Hudnut-Beumler, *In Pursuit of the Almighty's Dollar*.

[8]Rolland Allen, *Missionary Methods: St. Paul's or Ours?* (Grand Rapids: Eerdmans, 1962), p. 6.

[9]Ibid., p. 52.

[10]Andy Crouch, *Playing God: Redeeming the Gift of Power* (Downers Grove, IL: IVP Books, 2013), p. 34.

[11]Ibid., p. 35.

[12]The NRSV translates *kabash* "tread under foot" in this passage.

[13]Ralph Winter, "The 10 Super Centuries of Mission History," *Traveling Team,* accessed August 8, 2013, www.thetravelingteam.org/?q=node/88.

[14]C. S. Lewis, *The Weight of Glory and Other Addresses* (Grand Rapids: Eerdmans, 1949), p. 15.

[15]*Shalom* is a Hebrew word rich with the concept of flourishing. It integrates the concepts of peace, prosperity, completeness and welfare. Jeremiah 29:7 urges the Israelites to seek the shalom of Babylon. Various translations use "seek the peace and prosperity" (NIV), "seek the welfare" (NASB, NRSV, KJV) and "work for the country's welfare. Pray for Babylon's well-being" (*The Message*).

[16]E. Roels, *God's Mission: The Epistle to the Ephesians in Mission Perspective* (Franeker, Netherlands: Wever, 1962), p. 67, quoted in Anastasios Yannoulatos, "Purpose and Motive of Mission," *International Review of Missions* 54, no. 215 (1965): doi:10.1111/j.1758-6631.1965.tb01877.x.

[17]James J. Stamoolis, *Eastern Orthodox Mission Theology Today* (Maryknoll, NY: Orbis, 1986), p. 51.

[18]Dave Bookless, interview with author, August 20, 2013.

[19]From a personal interview with Lynn Green on August 21, 2013.

CHAPTER 5: FROM SOLITARY TO SOLIDARITY

[1]See Eric Brende, *Better Off: Flipping the Switch on Technology: Two People, One Year,*

Zero Watts (New York: HarperCollins, 2004).

[2]Thomas Cahill, *How the Irish Saved Civilization: The Untold Story of Ireland's Heroic Role from the Fall of Rome to the Rise of Medieval Europe* (New York: Anchor Books, 1995), p. 41.

[3]Monotheists comprise more than 50 percent of the global population, and over 80 percent of the earth's landmass hosts people of the three major monotheistic faiths— Christianity, Islam and Judaism.

[4]John Dyer, "Texas Bible (plugin): Fixing the Second Person Plural Problem One Website at a Time," Don't Eat the Fruit (personal website), May 24, 2013, http:// donteatthefruit.com/2013/05/texas-bible-second-person-plural-chrome-extension.

[5]Oddly enough, one of the biblical aspects of the modern corporation is that, under the law, a corporate entity is treated as an individual. The corporation can become a place where individuals share a sense of identity and destiny.

[6]Gretchen Anderson, "Loneliness Among Older Adults: A National Survey of Adults 45+," *AARP*, September 2010, www.aarp.org/personal-growth/transitions/info-09 -2010/loneliness_2010.html.

[7]James Joyner, "Record 28% of American Households One Person Only," *Outside the Beltway*, February 1, 2012, www.outsidethebeltway.com/record-28-of-american -households-one-person-only.

[8]James Hudnut-Beumler, *In Pursuit of the Almighty's Dollar: A History of Money and American Protestantism* (Chapel Hill: University of North Carolina Press, 2007), p. 33.

[9]E. Randolph Richards and Brandon J. O'Brien, *Misreading Scripture with Western Eyes: Removing Cultural Blinders to Better Understand the Bible* (Downers Grove, IL: IVP Books, 2012), p. 18.

[10]For a time-oriented person, church may begin at 10 a.m., for instance. An event-oriented person may, by contrast, believe church begins when a critical mass of people have arrived, regardless of the time. For more on a taxonomy of cultural values, see Marvin Mayers, *Christianity Confronts Culture: A Strategy for Cross-Cultural Evangelism* (Grand Rapids: Zondervan, 1987), pp. 157ff.

[11]Michael J. Sheeran, *Beyond Majority Rule: Voteless Decisions in the Religious Society of Friends* (West Chester, PA: Graphics Standard, 1996), p. 21.

[12]London Yearly Meeting, *Christian Faith and Practice*, 1960, par. 353, quoted in Sheeran, *Beyond Majority Rule,* p. 48.

[13]Philadelphia Yearly Meeting, *Faith and Practice*, 1972, pp. 17-18, quoted in Sheeran, *Beyond Majority Rule,* p. 48.

[14]Richards and J. O'Brien, *Misreading Scripture with Western Eyes,* p. 108.

[15]See "Corporate Personhood," *Wikipedia.com,* http://en.wikipedia.org/wiki/Corporate_personhood.

[16]Frank Viola and George Barna, *Pagan Christianity? Exploring the Roots of Our Church Practices* (Carol Stream, IL: Tyndale House, 2002), pp. 109ff.

[17]Again, for a more thoroughgoing argument, see ibid.

[18]Personal correspondence with the author.

CHAPTER 6: FROM MAINSTREAM TO MARGIN

[1]*Dalit* is an Indian term meaning "broken" or "oppressed." Dalits constitute an underclass within Indian society. Attracted to the egalitarian doctrine of Christianity, Dalits have adopted the Christian faith in droves, often as a communal decision-making process. Today more than two-thirds of all Indian Christians are believed to be Dalits, though they still suffer intense rejection and ostracism, even from higher-caste Indian Christians.

[2]"Many nations shall come and say: / 'Come, let us go up to the mountain of the LORD, / to the house of the God of Jacob; / that he may teach us his ways / and that we may walk in his paths'"(Micah 4:2).

[3]The mission of the Jesuits to the Guarani Indians of South America is a good example here. In his 1995 book *They Built Utopia: The Jesuit Missions in Paraguay 1610-1768,* Frederick Reiter traces the arc of 150 Jesuit communes built in the jungles of Paraguay, Uruguay and Brazil. There, Jesuit missionaries constructed utopic communities with shared wealth and relative peace, which were so prosperous that the colonial and magisterial church powers overtook the missions, confiscating their wealth and decimating their populations.

[4]Orlando E. Costas, *Christ Outside the Gate: Mission Beyond Christendom* (Eugene, OR: Wipf & Stock, 1982), p. 192.

[5]From the document of Betsey Stockton's official appointment, signed by Ashbel Green, Charles Samuel Stewart and Betsey Stockton, Princeton, October 24, 1822, and approved on behalf of the ABCFM by the Corresponding Secretary and Clerk of the Prudential Committee, Mr. Jeremiah Evarts. This document is in the archives of the ABCFM, Boston, and quoted in *Betsey Stockton: Pioneer American Missionary* (n.d.). The Free Library (2014). Available at www.thefreelibrary.com/Betsey+Stockton%3a+pioneer+American+missionary.-a016921617.

[6]Ashbel Green, *The Christian Advocate,* vol. 3, 1825, p. 39, available at http://books.google.com/books?id=_tk2AAAAMAAJ&source=gbs_navlinks_s.

Chapter 7: From Independent to Interdependent

[1]From correspondence with the author in September and October of 2013. Used with permission.

[2]Anomalies: Richard H. Thaler, Daniel Kahneman and Jack L. Knetsch, "The Endowment Effect, Loss Aversion, and Status Quo Bias," *The Journal of Economic Perspectives* 5, no. 1 (winter 1991): 193-206.

[3]Evan Lerner, "Penn Researchers Test Economic Theory Among Hunter-Gatherers," *Penn Current*, October 10 2013, www.upenn.edu/pennnews/current/2013-10-10/latest-news/penn-researchers-test-economic-theory-among-hunter-gatherers.

[4]See Robert Siegel and Shankar Vedantam, "Are We Genetically Inclined to Be Materialistic?" National Public Radio, December 26, 2013, www.npr.org/2013/12/26/257394308/are-we-genetically-inclined-to-be-materialistic.

[5]Raineer Chu, correspondence with the author in September and October of 2013.

[6]Andrew Carnegie, "The Problem of the Administration of Wealth," *The Gospel of Wealth and Other Timely Essays* (New York: Century, 1900).

[7]John C. Haughey, quoted in, *On Moral Business: Classical and Contemporary Resources for Ethics in Economic Life,* ed. Max L. Stackhouse (Grand Rapids: Eerdmans, 1995), p. 690.

[8]Brad Jersak, *Kissing the Leper: Seeing Jesus in the Least of These* (Abbotsford, BC: Fresh Wind Press, 2006).

[9]This story was recounted to me by Bob and Julio through prayer letters, phone calls and personal correspondence. Used with their permission.

[10]From correspondence with Jean-Luc Krieg. Shared with the permission of those being quoted.

Chapter 8: From Growth to Flourishing

[1]See "The Long Arm of Capitalist Structures" in the prologue.

[2]Kanzo Uchimura, "Can Americans Teach Japanese Religion?" *Japan Christian Intelligencer* 1 (1926): 257-61, quoted in Mark Noll, *The New Shape of World Christianity* (Downers Grove, IL: IVP Academic, 2009), pp. 88-89.

[3]Charles Spurgeon, *The Soul Winner: Or How to Lead Sinners to the Saviour* (New York: Fleming H. Revell, 1895), p. 13.

[4]See LifeChurch's video presentation titled "Because of You 2012," www.lifechurch.tv/2012review, accessed on August 23, 2013.

[5]Ibid.

[6]Professor Mathias Tomczak, "Science, Civilization and Society," Flinders University of South Australia, accessed August 25, 2013, www.es.flinders.edu.

au/~mattom/science+society/lecture3.html.

[7]See "Stress Statistics" at Statistic Brain, www.statisticbrain.com/stress-statistics.

[8]"Members of the clergy now suffer from obesity, hypertension and depression at rates higher than most Americans" (Paul Vitello, "Taking a Break from the Lord's Work," *New York Times*, August 1, 2010, www.nytimes.com/2010/08/02/nyregion/02burnout.html?pagewanted=all&_r=0).

ABOUT THE AUTHOR

Scott and his wife, Janine, live in Madison, Wisconsin, and have three children. Over the years they have enjoyed hosting many young people from all over the world with whom they have shared their home and their lives. They love encountering other cultures and have had the privilege of leading university students to a number of different locations.

Scott travels extensively as associate director of missions for InterVarsity Christian Fellowship. He oversees InterVarsity's work of mobilizing and equipping thousands of students each year who encounter God in challenging places throughout the United States and around the world. Since 2005 Scott has been spending a good deal of time with men and women who serve long term in developing world slum communities. He is author of *The New Friars: The Emerging Movement Serving the World's Poor* and *How to Inherit the Earth: Submitting Ourselves to a Servant Savior.* In addition, Scott has served as editor for *Quest for Hope in the Slum Community* and *Living Mission: The Vision and Voices of New Friars.*

Scott's great pet peeves include people who do not use their turn signals and those who return the ice cube tray to the freezer with only a couple of ice cubes remaining. He has a knack for picking the slowest lines and for hitting all the red lights, but only when he is in a hurry. Scott blogs at urbana.org and you can follow him on Twitter at @Bessenecker.